DATE DUE

SOCIAL SECURITY UNDER THE GUN

Also by Arthur Benavie:

Deficit Hysteria

SOCIAL SECURITY UNDER THE GUN

What Every Informed Citizen Needs to Know About Pension Reform

ARTHUR BENAVIE

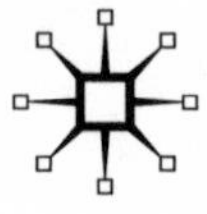

First published 2003 by
PALGRAVE MACMILLAN™
175 Fifth Avenue, New York, N.Y. 10010 and
Houndmills, Basingstoke, Hampshire, England RG21 6XS.
Companies and representatives throughout the world.

PALGRAVE MACMILLAN is the global academic imprint of the Palgrave Macmillan division of St. Martin's Press, LLC and of Palgrave Macmillan Ltd. Macmillan® is a registered trademark in the United States, United Kingdom and other countries. Palgrave is a registered trademark in the European Union and other countries.

ISBN 1–4039–6122–0 hardback

Library of Congress Cataloging-in-Publication Data
Benavie, Arthur.
Social security under the gun / by Arthur Benavie.
p. cm.
Includes bibliographical references.
ISBN 1–4039–6122–0
1. Social security—United States. 2. Social security—United States—Finance. 3. United States. Social Security Administration. I. Title.

HD7125.B367 2003
368.4'3'00973—dc21

2002029245

A catalogue record for this book is available from the British Library.

Design by Letra Libre, Inc.

First edition: January 2003
10 9 8 7 6 5 4 3 2 1

Printed in the United States of America.

To my wife, Marcy,
with all my love.

CONTENTS

ACKNOWLEDGMENTS

I am grateful to Ed Baxter, Richard Froyen, and Bill Schweke for their helpful comments on an earlier version of this book.

I am also thankful to my editor, Anthony Wahl, for his valuable suggestions, along with his enthusiasm and encouragement.

Without question, though, my greatest debt of gratitude is to my wife, Marcy Lansman, who spent many weeks working with me on the manuscript. To the extent that the text is lucid and well organized, she deserves much of the credit.

INTRODUCTION

Worried Social Security won't be around when you retire? Scared it will have failed by the time your children are ready to draw on it? You're not alone. A huge proportion of Americans have been convinced that the Social Security system is collapsing, that it can't survive without a major overhaul. The purpose of this book is to examine these claims and take a look at proposed solutions.

Attacks on Social Security have escalated in the 1990s, along with tributes praising it as the most successful domestic program in American history. Though Main Street still supports Social Security, Wall Street (and many analysts advising Congress) want to drastically change it. Two types of reform are being proposed. One is privatization—permitting wage earners to divert a portion of their payroll taxes into personal retirement accounts that can be invested in the stock market. The other is allowing the government to invest a portion of the Social Security trust fund in the stock market.

Either of these reforms would constitute a fundamental restructuring of our public pension system. Under privatization, a slice of the core retirement income of future workers would be directly affected by the ups and downs of the stock market. (Social Security benefits now are guaranteed by law.) Allowing the trust fund to be invested in stocks would make the federal government a major owner of private industry.

Do we really need such basic reforms? Supporters say yes, for several reasons. According to the reformers:

- Social Security is heading for bankruptcy.
- Our children will be impoverished supporting the elderly.
- The return on our payroll taxes is too low and falling.
- All wage earners should have access to the stock market, even the poor.
- Americans should have the freedom to handle their own retirement savings.

The goal of this book is to spell out the arguments for and against restructuring Social Security.

Clashing values and passionate emotions characterize this debate. Scholars act like politicians as they throw brickbats at each other in otherwise esoteric tomes. My objective here is not to convert you to one position or the other but to lay out the issues as fairly and clearly as I can. To help you decide where you stand on the issues, I'll distinguish the economic relationships from the personal value judgments. There is remarkable unanimity among economists concerning the economics of Social Security. The disagreements stem mostly from conflicting social philosophies.

Beware of leaving this controversy to the politicians. Trite as it sounds, the right decisions won't be made unless you, the public, are informed and politically active. The good news is that the subject is accessible. Furthermore, there is no such thing as a scientifically correct solution. The key question is: What kind of public pension system do you want? There is no higher authority here.

VALUES UNDERLYING SOCIAL SECURITY

Social Security is based on the principle of *social insurance:* You pay premiums (payroll taxes) so that the government will pay you benefits in the event that a particular problem (e.g., disability) or condition (e.g., retirement in old age) occurs. In other words, the government protects you and your family from destitution as a result of retirement, disability, or death of a breadwinner. You are required by law to have payroll taxes deducted from your paycheck during your working life in order to earn the right to Social Security benefits. Coverage is almost universal.

Our system is mainly pay-as-you-go. That is, payroll taxes contributed by current wage earners are handed over to current beneficiaries. Currently (2002) about 75 percent of the revenue flowing into Social Security is used to pay benefits, with the remainder going into a trust fund. Given the current payroll tax rate, revenue will start to fall short of benefits a few years after the baby boomers begin to retire in 2010. Then the assets in the trust fund will begin to be drawn down. According to the current official projection, the Social Security Trust Fund will be depleted by 2041.[1]

Two values lie at the heart of Social Security: *adequacy* and *equity. Adequacy* means no worker who has paid into the system over a lifetime should wind up in poverty. *Equity* means the more people put in, the more they should get out. The formula used to compute Social Security benefits embodies both of these principles. Higher income contributors receive a higher monthly benefit than lower income contributors, but not proportionately so. That is, if, over your working life, you have paid twice the payroll taxes I have, you will get higher Social Security benefits than I do, but not twice as high. This redistribution of income from the rich to the poor reflects an attempt to satisfy the adequacy principle.

Unfortunately, the adequacy objective has not been achieved. For example, single individuals who have worked for 35 years at the minimum wage will earn Social Security benefits that put them below the poverty line.

Some analysts have questioned whether, overall, Social Security does redistribute income from the rich to the poor, since lower income people tend to have shorter life spans and thus receive fewer benefit checks. But, as the Congressional Budget Office has pointed out, "Social Security also provides benefits to the survivors of deceased workers and to disabled workers; both of those features contribute to the program's progressivity [that is, support for low-income workers]."[2] Most scholars believe that Social Security has done more to eliminate poverty among the elderly than any other government program, including welfare. During the past 30 years, thanks largely to the expansion of Social Security, the poverty rate among the elderly has dropped from about three times that of the general population to about the same.[3] It has been estimated that Social Security keeps around 15 million people out of poverty and millions more out of near poverty.[4] Two out of five retirees receive over 75 percent of their income from Social Security.[5] As the economist Edward Gramlich, chair of the Social Security Advisory Council, put it, "Social Security is still far and away the nation's most significant antipoverty program."[6]

Social Security is not welfare. People have earned the right to their Social Security benefits by paying their payroll taxes. By contrast, welfare programs—such as Medicaid, food stamps, and supplemental security income—are *means-tested;* that is, a person has only to be certified as sufficiently poor in order to be eligible. Social Security is not means-tested. Even the richest get benefits. Thus, America's approach to old-age security is based primarily on the principles of social insurance, not welfare.

In 1935, the founders of Social Security based the program on payroll taxes rather than means-testing in order to guarantee the long-term survival of the program. President Franklin D. Roosevelt, talking privately to an advisor, put his rationale this way: "We put those payroll contributions there so as to give the contributors a legal, moral and political right to collect their pensions. . . . With those taxes in there, no damn politician can ever scrap my Social Security program."[7]

According to the historian Edward Berkowitz, "Roosevelt took as his major premise the corrosive effects of welfare on the human spirit" and "saw in social insurance an uplifting rather than a soul-destroying program."[8]

Wilbur Cohen, a former secretary of Health, Education, and Welfare, played a major role in the development of Social Security for almost 50 years. Cohen said of means-testing versus social insurance: "A program that deals only with the poor will end up being a poor program. . . . And a program that is only for the poor—one that has nothing in it for the middle income and upper income—is, in the long run, a program the American public won't support."[9]

OTHER FEATURES OF THE PROGRAM

Here are some other characteristics of Social Security that are rarely mentioned by the news media:[10]

- The cost of administering the program is extremely low—less than 1 percent of the value of the benefits it pays out, compared with 10 to 15 percent for most private insurance.
- Social Security payments are automatically protected against inflation. As far as I know, this benefit is not available privately—that is, private pensions do not yet protect against inflation that

is *unanticipated.* The purchasing power of the fixed monthly benefit promised by most private pension plans erodes over time as prices rise. For example, if the average price level rises 3 percent a year, the purchasing power of a fixed monthly benefit is cut almost in half in 20 years. If the price level rises 2 percent a year, the fixed benefit loses over one third of its purchasing power in 20 years. Thanks to the cost-of-living adjustment (COLA), Social Security benefits retain their purchasing power throughout the life of the beneficiary.

- Social Security provides support to families who lose income as a result of the death or disability of a breadwinner, protection many families would be unable to buy privately. As of January 2001, Social Security paid monthly survivor benefits to about 7 million Americans, including 2 million children. Disability benefits were paid to 5 million workers under age 65 and 1.6 million dependents, most of whom were children. About 28 million retired workers receive monthly benefits, as do 12 million family members of retired, disabled, or deceased workers.[11]
- The disability coverage provided by Social Security does not require extra premiums. It's covered by payroll taxes. Social Security has the advantage of being mandatory and almost universal. There is no *adverse selection* as there is with many kinds of private insurance. (Adverse selection refers to the fact that sick people are more likely to buy health coverage, thus driving up the cost.)
- Unlike many private pension plans, Social Security is portable. It follows you from job to job.

Social Security is a mechanism for sharing the cost of providing for the disabled and the elderly. Because of Social Security, few of the elderly have to move in with their children. As Robert Ball puts it, "Through Social Security we recognize that 'we're all in this together.'"[12]

IS SOCIAL SECURITY GOING BANKRUPT?

According to the Social Security and Medicare trustees, revenue taken in over the next 75 years will fall short of required expenditures given the current law.[13] (Seventy-five years is simply the traditional long-run time frame employed by the actuaries.) Assuming we retain the current system, we will have to either raise revenue or cut benefits to make ends meet. The problem is not here yet, however. These days the system is rolling in money. The crunch is projected to come about four decades in the future.

No one questions the skills or the integrity of the trustees, but a projection like this is an educated guess, which could be miles off the mark and often is. It's based on a battery of assumptions, each of which is also an educated guess, about future births, deaths, interest rates, wage rates, productivity, immigration, and health care costs. As the trustees themselves say, "Any estimates for as long as 75 years into the future are inherently uncertain."[14]

Even short-run projections are treacherous. Consider the recent embarrassment of the Congressional Budget Office (CBO). In January 1997, the CBO predicted that the budget deficit for 1999 would be $148 billion. Six months later it predicted a surplus of $125 billion, a difference of more than a quarter of a trillion dollars![15] (The CBO is staffed with professional economists and is the research arm for both Democrats and Republicans in the U.S. Congress, so no one doubts that its forecasts are honest and competent.)

One way to measure the revenue shortfall predicted by the Social Security trustees is to estimate the amount by which we would have to raise payroll taxes in order to eliminate it. To make Social Security revenue equal benefits over the next 75 years, we could raise the payroll tax rate now by about 2 percentage points, from 12.4 percent to 14.4 percent (1 percentage point on workers and 1 percentage point on employers).[16] Doing so would still leave the United States among the most lightly taxed industrial countries in the world.[17]

WHAT IS THE SOCIAL SECURITY TRUST FUND?

Pundits like to say the Social Security trust fund is going bankrupt. This alarming prediction has caused many people to fear that their payroll taxes are going down a rat hole, that they will never see any benefits.

What does it mean to say the trust fund is going bankrupt? To understand and evaluate this statement you have to know how the Social Security trust fund works.[18]

Suppose a rich relative sets up a $100,000 trust fund and names you as the beneficiary. You are in some sense $100,000 richer. You could eventually use the income from the trust fund to buy a car or pay for a vacation in Bermuda. The analogy between your trust fund and the Social Security trust fund is misleading. Though your trust fund constitutes a source of wealth that you can draw on, this is not true of the Social Security trust fund. Its assets are an accounting fiction, an illusion that results from the way the U.S. Treasury does its bookkeeping, nothing more than IOUs from the government to the government.

Perhaps the best way to explain is to imagine a family that uses the same peculiar accounting procedure. Suppose this family earmarks a fraction of its income for medical bills and deposits that money in a special checking account. If family members incur medical expenses less than those earmarked, they "borrow" the excess and spend it on other things, leaving IOUs in the flap of the checkbook in place of the borrowed funds. Do these IOUs enable the family to meet its future medical expenses? Of course not. Their ability to come up with the money depends on the their future income.

The U.S. Treasury behaves like this family. It has set up a special account called the trust fund to pay Social Security expenses. All revenue earmarked for Social Security is credited to this account, and all benefits are debited. Whenever Social Security revenue exceeds benefits, the Treasury spends the surplus for congressionally approved, non–Social Security purposes and leaves behind its IOUs—Treasury bonds. The stock of these Treasury bonds constitutes the trust fund balance (or assets).

Many people are angry that the Treasury uses excess payroll taxes to fund non–Social Security expenditures. You frequently hear that the Treasury is "raiding the Trust Fund" by spending these surpluses. Newt Gingrich, former Speaker of the House, put it this way:

> The money the government supposedly has been putting aside from the baby boomers' Social Security taxes *is not there.* The government has been borrowing the money. . . . So, when the baby boomers get set to retire, where's the money to pay them going to come from?[19]

Gingrich was right. The Treasury *has* borrowed the Social Security surplus. The money *isn't* there. Why did the Treasury do that? It was required to by law. Any excess Social Security revenue must go to the Treasury in exchange for Treasury bonds. (We usually say the Social Security surplus must be "invested" in Treasury bonds.) The Treasury must use these surplus funds on congressionally authorized programs, or, if there is surplus in the overall government budget, it will use the money to retire the public debt.

When Social Security revenue falls short of benefits, the Treasury must rustle up the needed money. The accounting procedure has it buying back its own IOUs, diminishing Social Security's trust fund balance.

If the IOUs go to zero, the trust fund assets are said to be exhausted, or as the news media like to put it, the trust fund is "bankrupt." Does that mean Social Security has to cut benefits? Not necessarily. Payroll taxes will continue to roll in and may or may not cover the scheduled benefits. If future taxes fell short, Congress would have to act, either cutting benefits or raising Social Security revenue.

So what's the purpose of the trust fund assets? They are a record of the accumulated payroll taxes the Treasury has borrowed from the trust fund and used for non–Social Security purposes. They constitute the debt the Treasury owes Social Security. As economist Barbara Bergmann put it, "The bonds in the Trust Fund represent a formal promise that the Treasury will send a certain amount of money to the Social Security agency when Social Security taxes don't cover benefits."[20]

If the Social Security Trust Fund does become depleted in 2041, will this be the first time its balance has gone to zero? Hardly. For the half century following the creation of Social Security in 1935, the assets in the trust fund were negligible because payroll tax rates were adjusted so that revenue equaled benefits. Yet no one screamed that Social Security was bankrupt. The financial problem currently facing Social Security is not that the assets in the trust fund will be exhausted. It is that over the next 75 years revenues dedicated to Social Security are projected to cover only about 70 percent of promised benefits. Various solutions to this long-run deficit have been proposed. I will examine them in chapter 1.

THE COST OF SUPPORTING THE FUTURE ELDERLY

Like horror stories? Then you'd love some of the books about Social Security. They'll scare the hell out of you. Let me suggest a thriller by a well known economist, Peter Peterson, a former secretary of Commerce, chair of a leading investment bank, and advisor to presidents from Nixon to Clinton. In *Will America Grow Up Before It Grows Old?* (subtitled "How the Coming Social Security Crisis Threatens You, Your Family, and Your Country"), Peterson argues that disaster is inevitable unless we radically reform Social Security by privatization and by denying benefits to the well-to-do. Here's a typical paragraph:

> The economist—and sometimes humorist—Herbert Stein likes to say, "If something is unsustainable, it tends to stop." Or as the old adage advises, "If your horse dies, we suggest you dismount." We cannot finance the unfinanceable. By the year 2013, as Baby Boomers retire en masse, the annual surplus of Social Security tax revenues over outlays will disappear, and turn negative, By 2030, when all the Boomers will have reached sixty-five, Social Security will be running an *annual* cash deficit of $766 billion. If Medicare Hospital Insurance is included and if both programs continue according to current law, the combined cash deficit that year will be $1.7 trillion. The horse, in other words, will be quite dead.[21]

Scared? I don't blame you. Are Peterson's projections correct? They're as good as we have. But his message is misleading because he tells only half the story. He describes the increasing burden of supporting the elderly, but he ignores the fact that our ability to support them will also be growing. Just as your debts are backed by your income, our debt to seniors is backed by our nation's income.

To assess how burdensome this debt will be, we need to relate it to our national income. The most common measure of national income is the gross domestic product (GDP), which is the total value of income earned in the United States. As Social Security and Medicare payments grow over the next several decades, so will the GDP. These payments are expected to grow faster than the GDP, however, because our population is aging. Therefore, meeting payments owed to seniors will likely require an increase in the tax rate. In other words, to eliminate the deficits Peterson describes, taxes will have to increase as a fraction of GDP. Currently these payments to seniors are around 7 percent of GDP. In 2050, the official estimate is that the payments to seniors will run about 12 percent of GDP, and in 2073 about 12.75 percent.[22] So our tax burden to support the elderly will almost double over the next 70 years if we maintain the current benefit schedules.

Will our children and grandchildren be impoverished supporting the elderly? Using an extremely cautious assumption, the average income per worker (adjusted for inflation) will double by 2073.[23] So if you currently earn $50,000 a year, your grandchild (or great-grandchild) will earn at least $100,000 a year (in today's prices) in 2073. Of your income of $50,000, 7 percent is taxed to pay for the retirement and health needs of the elderly, leaving you with $46,500. In 2073, your grandchild will have to pay 12.75 percent of her salary to support the aged, which leaves her with $87,250. Your grandchild will thus be almost twice as rich as you are, even after subtracting the higher taxes necessary to pay for Social Security and Medicare.[24]

What *should* the future tax rate be to support the elderly? Economics can't give you an answer to that, because a change in the tax burden involves gainers and losers, and there is no scientific way of measuring the loser's pain against the gainer's pleasure. The decision as to how much of the nation's pie should go to the elderly is a value judgment. Economists are in agreement, however, that over the long run the GDP per capita will grow, as it always has. So, even with no restructuring of our Social Security system, both future workers and retirees could be better off than we are.

MAIN STREET'S VIEW OF SOCIAL SECURITY

The media thrive on the lurid and sensational. Sex and violence are the usual fare, but Social Security is moving up fast. Pundits would have us believe the public has lost all confidence in the program. Journalists—incorrectly interpreting survey data—have reported that young Americans think they are more likely to see a UFO than to collect Social Security benefits.[25] A *New Republic* cover shows the words "UH-OH" replacing the number on a huge Social Security card. "Social Security Is on the Skids," the caption reads. A *USA Today* story reports that 60 percent of Americans are demanding their "money's worth" and want to "invest some of their Social Security taxes themselves."[26] More generally, the media warn that the growing burden of Social Security will lead to intergenerational warfare, with the young perceiving their parents as greedy geezers.[27]

Is this portrayal a fair representation of public opinion? Here's what opinion research tells us: Support for Social Security has remained stable and high over the past two and a half decades, but confidence has fluctuated.[28] Between 1976 and 1982, confidence plummeted from 60 percent to 32 percent, deflated by alarming news coverage, worries about inflation, and a growing distrust of government. After adjustments were made in 1983 to stave off a financial emergency, confidence edged back up until around 1990, then declined again through the 1990s as the attacks on the program escalated.

Throughout this entire period, support for Social Security remained steadfast. For example, in a series of polls taken from 1984 through 1997, 87 percent or more of respondents reported they believed funding for Social Security was either just right or too *low.* In a 1999 survey, 94 percent of respondents expressed their support for Social Security by agreeing that it was important to make the program financially sound.[29]

The young are strong supporters of Social Security, often more so than their elders.[30] In a March 1997 *Washington Post* survey, the young were more concerned than other respondents that retirement benefits were too low. A February 1997 *Los Angeles Times* survey found that the young were more supportive than their elders of the Social Security system. A 1996 survey showed that 63 percent of Americans were willing to spend tax revenues on benefits for well-to-do seniors, with the young more supportive than the elderly.

Why are young Americans such hardy supporters of Social Security? Opinion research shows that young people understand that Social Security is insurance against poverty in retirement and that it is a right that has been earned during working years. They see canceling benefits as breaking a promise. In addition, they count on Social Security to help support their retired parents. Surveys have confirmed that "three-quarters of Americans supported Social Security because it relieved them of the financial burden of caring for their parents."[31]

Americans have reported they have little objection to the Social Security payroll tax. Four out of five said they felt the tax was fair and they knew it was used mostly to pay current benefits. Almost two thirds said they would be willing to pay higher taxes if benefits were in danger of being cut.[32]

Pollsters who ask whether people would like to invest some of their Social Security payroll taxes in the stock market get an enthusiastic "yes," especially from young and better educated respondents. But such questions often neglect to mention the costs of privatization, such as the risk of losing money in the stock market and the additional taxes necessary to replace lost revenue. Posing the survey question so that respondents are made aware of these costs results in a rejection of privatization by more than 3 to 1.[33]

Several Democrats have proposed to reform Social Security by investing part of the trust fund in the stock market. Survey respondents have overwhelmingly rejected this idea. For example, in the NPR/Kaiser/Kennedy School survey of May 20, 1999, 61 percent opposed and 38 percent supported "having the government invest in the private stock market a portion of Social Security reserve funds, which are currently invested in government bonds."[34]

To summarize: During the 1990s a majority of Americans of all ages supported Social Security and rejected the idea of investing payroll taxes in the stock market. During that same period, politicians and academics put forth a flood of proposals recommending that payroll taxes be invested in the stock market.[35] Why the disconnect between the public on one hand and politicians and scholars on the other? One factor may be an elitist bias on the part of politicians and scholars, who normally retire with a healthy nest egg. Social Security constitutes only a fraction of their retirement income, so they can afford to play the stock market with it. If this gamble should expose them to more risk then they find comfortable, they can reshuffle the assets in the rest of their portfolio. An additional factor may be that some politicians believe retirement income can be increased without increasing taxes if payroll taxes are diverted into personal retirement accounts that can be invested in the stock market. This reasoning is flawed. I explain why in chapter 2.

WHY THE PRESSURE TO REFORM SOCIAL SECURITY?

In 1982, Social Security faced an immediate financial crisis: revenue was insufficient to cover benefits. President Reagan set up a blue ribbon commission headed by Alan Greenspan to solve the problem. The commission's recommendations were quickly enacted by Congress. The rescue package consisted of tax increases and benefit cuts; specifically, Congress postponed the cost-of-living adjustment for six months, increased the payroll tax, extended coverage to more workers, and subjected a portion of the Social Security benefits of high-income individuals to the income tax.[36] As for fundamentally restructuring Social Security, the commission explicitly said no.[37]

After 20 years, analysts and politicians are no longer satisfied with simply raising revenue and cutting benefits. Now they're pressing for more basic reforms, such as privatization or the investment of the trust fund in the stock market. Why the change?

For one thing, there is no immediate financial crisis, just a projected long-run deficit. Were we facing an emergency as we were in 1982, we wouldn't have the leisure to argue over the philosophy of Social Security. We would be forced to act fast, as the Greenspan commission did, in devising the least painful ways of eliminating the shortfall. On the other hand, if Social Security had enough money now and was projected to have enough in the future, anyone arguing for restructuring the most popular domestic program in American history would sound like a crank or worse. Today we have the perfect climate for those who dislike the values reflected in the current system: a crisis looming in the fairly distant future with plenty of time to critique the current program and consider fundamental reforms.

At the heart of the debate over Social Security are values, not economic facts. That's why the conflicts are so emotional and why there's no consensus, even among the experts. Two visions are in conflict here, and both have an honored place in American tradition. One sees a society in which individuals look after themselves, are responsible for their lives, and have freedom to make their own decisions. Through this lens Social Security looks paternalistic. It forcibly extracts money from workers and doles it back to them during their retirement. It's easy to understand the disgruntled citizen who says, "How about letting me handle my own money? I can do a lot better than the government, and whatever happens, I'll take the consequences."

The vision embodied in Social Security clashes with this view. According to this vision, society is a family responsible for its members.

Risks are shared. The cost of caring for the elderly and the disabled is spread over the entire society. The highest earners contribute the most. The less fortunate receive help. Social Security assumes responsibilities that used to be borne by families, which have become increasingly dispersed during the past century. Under Social Security, the elderly are no longer forced to move in with their children. Thanks to Social Security, they can live independently.

In 1994, Health and Human Services Secretary Donna Shalala appointed a panel of 13 experts to form the Advisory Council on Social Security, the mission of which was to recommend changes that would bring Social Security into long-term solvency. Even after three years, the Advisory Council had not reached consensus. Members' differences reflected the tension between the values of individual freedom and collective responsibility. The panel split into three groups. Two of the groups, adding up to seven members, proposed privatizing Social Security, although there were major differences between their two plans. The third group, of six members, recommended maintaining the current system but favored investing a portion of the trust fund in the stock market.

In this book I examine the pros and cons of these reform proposals and develop the background you'll need to decide where you stand in the Social Security debate.

PLAN OF THE BOOK

CHAPTER 1. FIXING SOCIAL SECURITY

Social Security faces two major problems: projected revenue will be insufficient to pay benefits over the next several decades, and the rate of return on our payroll taxes is perceived as too low and is predicted to be even lower for future generations. In chapter 1, I argue that these problems can be solved without fundamentally restructuring Social Security and evaluate several proposals that would do so.

Chapter 2. Should We Privatize Social Security?

To argue that Social Security's problems can be solved without changing its structure is not to say that basic reform is undesirable. In chapter 2, I discuss the advantages and disadvantages of diverting a portion of the payroll tax into personal retirement accounts that could be invested in the stock market. I also examine the two countries—Britain and Chile—that have had some experience with privatization and assess the relevance of their experience for the United States.

Chapter 3. Diversifying the Trust Fund

Another possible reform would be to allow the Social Security trust fund to be invested in the stock market. Currently, excess revenue must by law be invested in Treasury bonds. The argument for loosening these restrictions is that over the long run private stocks generally earn more than government bonds. In chapter 3, I evaluate diversification and examine a plan that would increase trust fund earnings without incurring the political risks of allowing the government to hold a huge portfolio of private assets.

Chapter 4. Questions and Answers

I suggest answers to the questions you may be faced with when your friends find out you've read this book.

CHAPTER ONE

FIXING SOCIAL SECURITY

Social Security faces two major problems: a shortage of revenue over the long run and the public's perception that the rate of return on payroll taxes is too low. Many politicians, columnists, and scholars assume that the only way to solve these problems is to fundamentally restructure the program by diverting a portion of the payroll tax into personal retirement accounts and giving workers the option of investing these funds in the stock market. This reasoning has become widely accepted during the last several years. As Representative E. Clay Shaw Jr. (R-FL), chair of the House Ways and Means Social Security Subcommittee, put it: "The question is, should you have individual accounts in addition to the existing system. You have to. There is no other way to save Social Security for our children and grandchildren."[1]

President George W. Bush also wants privatization: "We must save Social Security. . . . In my address to Congress, I described the principles that must guide any reform. . . . Social Security reform must offer personal savings accounts to younger workers who want them."[2]

To me this logic seems flawed—almost as irrational as saying that because your house needs a new roof you have to buy another house. *The problems facing Social Security do not require that it be fundamentally reformed by diverting payroll taxes into the stock market. Perhaps we can do better by tuning Social Security up rather than trading it in.*

In this chapter, I discuss ways of solving Social Security's problems without altering its basic structure.

REMEDIES FOR THE LONG-RUN DEFICIT

According to official projections, Social Security needs additional revenue over the next several decades in order to pay benefits that have been promised.[3] How serious is this problem? The Social Security trustees don't seem alarmed. They said in their 1999 report that the problem "can be solved by small gradual changes." The Advisory Council agreed, saying that the long run deficit can be taken care of "without much difficulty by making several relatively minor changes."[4]

How can we eliminate this shortfall without fundamentally restructuring Social Security? A variety of proposals to raise revenue or cut benefits have been offered by analysts and politicians.[5] The ideas currently being debated include

- making Social Security universal
- altering the benefit formula
- raising the payroll tax cap
- raising the tax on benefits
- cutting the COLA (the cost-of-living adjustment)
- lengthening the period for averaging wages

- increasing the normal retirement age
- means-testing

In addition, we could simply raise the payroll tax rate. This tax does, however, weigh disproportionately on low income families, and polls indicate that the American people are against boosting it by almost two to one.[6]

Making Social Security Universal

Social Security currently covers 96 percent of all wage earners, but about a quarter of all state and local government workers (around 4 million) are left out.[7] Bringing in all newly hired state and local workers would help solve the long-term deficit because these wage earners would pay payroll taxes for many years before receiving benefits. To include all state and local government workers hired after 2000 would reduce the long-term deficit by an estimated 11 percent.[8]

This idea, unanimously supported by the Advisory Council, has generated little controversy and is a part of most reform plans.[9] It is widely agreed that all wage earners should be a part of the nation's social insurance program. Though the tax burden on presently excluded state and local government workers would rise, they would benefit as well, since they would have greater freedom to change jobs without losing benefits, better protection against inflation, better survivor and disability coverage, and more reliable protection for spouses who are not automatically protected under state plans.

Altering the Benefit Formula

Given the current Social Security system, your children's benefits will almost surely be greater than yours, even adjusting for inflation. Why is this? Because of the way Social Security benefits are calculated. They're computed using a formula by which the monthly benefit equals some percentage of lifetime average monthly wage. The higher the average wage, the higher the benefit. Specifically, according to the formula used in 2002, a worker's monthly Social Security benefit equaled 90 percent of that worker's first $592 of average monthly earnings, plus 32 percent of the next $2,975, plus 15 percent of the earnings between $3,381 and $6,700.[10] These earnings numbers are scheduled to rise each year to keep pace with prices. (Earnings exceeding $6,700 were neither taxed nor included in the benefits formula.) Note that the benefit formula is constructed so that benefits of higher income workers constitute a smaller percentage of their lifetime average monthly income than benefits of lower income workers. This formula is largely responsible for the anti-poverty effects of Social Security.

In the economy as a whole, the average wage has always tended to move upward over time, even adjusting for inflation. As a result the purchasing power of Social Security benefits has increased from one generation to the next. Experts predict that this trend will continue.

The Social Security deficit could be reduced by altering the benefit formula so that benefits would continue to rise over time but at a slower pace. This idea is embodied in a proposal by Edward Gramlich, chair of the 1994–1996 Advisory Council, and also in the plan presented by the National Commission on Retirement Policy, a commission consisting of Senators John Breaux (D-LA) and Judd Gregg (R-NH) and Representatives Jim Kolbe (R-AZ) and Charles Stenholm (D-TX).[11]

The idea has stirred little controversy, perhaps because the formula can be adjusted so that most of the benefit cuts are focused on the wealthy. Although 90 percent of Americans oppose an across the board cut in benefits, almost three out of five support a reduction for those with incomes of more than $40,000 a year.[12]

If the benefit formula were gradually adjusted so that the purchasing power of future benefits equaled that of those now being paid to new beneficiaries, the long run deficit would be reduced by around 9 percent.[13]

Raising the Payroll Tax Cap

It doesn't matter whether your annual salary is $80,000 or $800,000 or $8 million, you pay the same Social Security tax (currently $4,724 per year) because wages above a certain level are ignored by the Social Security system: they are neither subject to the payroll tax (currently 6.2 percent of wage income) nor included in the benefits formula.[14] In 2001, that maximum wage level—called the payroll tax cap—was $80,400. This maximum wage is scheduled to go up every year to keep pace with increases in the nation's average wage.

Raising the cap would increase both revenues and benefits, but it would increase revenues more. For example, raising the cap by 2 percent a year above the already scheduled increases would reduce the long-term deficit by around 12 percent.[15]

Why not eliminate the cap altogether and require people to pay Social Security taxes on their entire wage income? Shouldn't a corporation president earning a salary of $8 million a year pay a higher payroll tax than I do? This sounds like a good idea when we look at only the revenue side. The rub comes on the benefit side. Do we want to give multimillionaires Social Security benefits that run to six figures?

The reason the cap has been retained is political. As economist Wallace Peterson put it, eliminating the cap "would be strongly resisted by higher-income wage and salary workers, for their taxes would rise more than their benefits."[16] Researchers Dean Baker and Mark Weisbrot agreed, predicting a "backlash among upper income taxpayers" if the cap were lifted.[17]

Most reform plans supported by Democrats would raise the cap faster than is presently scheduled.[18] For example, the plan endorsed by Senators Daniel Patrick Moynihan (D-NY) and J. Robert Kerrey (D-NE) would increase the cap to $96,600 by 2003 instead of $82,800 as scheduled. Plans advanced by Republicans don't even mention the cap.[19]

Raising the Tax on Benefits

Income taxes on Social Security benefits—unlike income taxes on other types of income—are credited to the Social Security trust fund. Thus, raising the tax on benefits would help solve Social Security's revenue shortfall.

Currently, we tax Social Security benefits less heavily than we do private pensions.[20] This disparity violates the widely accepted principle that equal incomes should be taxed equally. There is general agreement that this disparity should be eliminated. As the Advisory Council put it, "The fairest way to ask present retirees to share in the cost of bringing Social Security into balance is by revising the taxation of Social Security benefits."[21]

Payments from private pension plans are subject to the income tax only to the extent that they exceed the amount workers have paid in. This portion of the income tax is computed on an individual basis. By contrast, Social Security benefits are taxed at a rate of 85 percent across the board except for low-income taxpayers. (Congress set the 85 percent figure to serve as an estimate of benefits that exceed payroll taxes a worker has paid into the system.)

Economists are critical of the 85 percent formula. They argue that the procedure used to compute income taxes on Social Security benefits should be the same as that used to compute taxes on private pensions, individual by individual. Such a procedure would not only be fair, it would boost Social Security revenue; and the Advisory Council has concluded that "the administrative difficulty of individual calculation is manageable."[22]

There is another difference between the taxation of private pension payments and that of Social Security benefits: benefits received by low-income workers are exempt from the income tax, whereas private pension payments are not. Currently, beneficiaries with annual incomes less than $34,000 for single persons and $44,000 for couples are exempt from income tax on Social Security benefits. Most experts agree that this special exemption should be eliminated, that low-income beneficiaries should be given only the protection provided to all low-income taxpayers.

If the tax on Social Security benefits were computed on an individual basis and if the special exemption were eliminated, the long run deficit would be cut by around 16 percent.[23]

Cutting the Cost-of-Living Adjustment (COLA)

Question: How many types of retirement income are automatically adjusted for inflation?
Answer: Only one—Social Security.

Savings accounts are eroded by rising price levels. So are private pensions, since corporations do not insure their retired workers against the ravages of *unexpected* inflation.

As Henry Aaron and Robert Reischauer put it, "Social Security remains the only source of retirement income that is insulated from the risk of unanticipated inflation and guaranteed to continue as long as the pensioners live."[24] (Henry Aaron was chair of the 1979 Advisory Council, and Robert Reischauer was director of the CBO from 1989 to 1995.)

In 1972, Congress adopted a formula to adjust Social Security benefits automatically, tying them to the consumer price index (CPI); that is, if the CPI rose by, say, 3 percent, benefits would automatically rise by 3 percent. This cost-of-living adjustment (COLA) was intended to guarantee that the purchasing power of benefits would be immune to inflation. Statisticians at the Bureau of Labor Statistics are charged with the task of computing the consumer price index.

When politicians are under pressure to cut spending, one place they look is the COLA.[25] For example, lowering the growth rate in the consumer price index by .2 percent per year would cut Social Security benefits and reduce the long-run deficit by approximately 13 percent. It was for this reason that the Boskin Commission was appointed by the Senate Finance Committee in 1996 to evaluate the accuracy of the consumer price index. It was chaired by Michael Boskin, who had been top economic advisor for the elder President George Bush. At that time the United States was experiencing huge budget deficits that forecasters predicted would continue indefinitely. Politicians were desperate to reduce spending. Trimming the COLA would do the job, at the expense of Social Security beneficiaries. The commission, which consisted of five economists who had already testified they believed the consumer price index overestimated inflation, concluded that it overstated inflation by 1.1 percent a year and recommended cutting the COLA and therefore Social Security benefits by a corresponding amount.[26] (The Bureau of Labor Statistics disagreed.) One percent may not sound like much, but a COLA reduction of this size would reduce benefits by more than 10 percent over an average 20-year retirement.[27]

The Boskin Commission's conclusion, although rejected by many economists, has influenced policy makers.[28] Many reform plans, such as the Moynihan and the Kerrey-Simpson proposals, have incorporated the commission's recommendation.

Economists, however, are in general agreement that the computation of the consumer price index should remain a technical one, left to the Bureau of Labor Statistics, and that it should not become a political football. Even the Advisory Council, which had heated and unbridgeable disagreements over how to reform Social Security, agreed unanimously that the COLA should be determined by the Bureau of Labor Statistics and should not be "motivated by political considerations."[29]

In 1996 the Bureau of Labor Statistics announced that it had improved the consumer price index, making it a more accurate measure of inflation. This change reduces the COLA and will shrink the long run deficit by an estimated 19 percent.[30]

Lengthening the Period for Averaging Wages

Social Security benefits are determined by a worker's average annual salary, an average based on the 35 years of highest earnings.[31] A wage earner must have paid payroll taxes for at least 10 years to be eligible. However, if a person with less than 10 years' work experience is the spouse of a worker who is entitled to Social Security, then the spouse, when 65, receives 50 percent of the worker's benefits. The same option holds for a person with more than 10 years' work experience if the 50 percent benefit exceeds his or her own full benefit. If a person has worked, say, 12 years, the average wage would be calculated using the wage incomes for those 12 years plus 23 zeros.

A majority of the Advisory Council and many reform plans have recommended increasing the number of years used to compute the average wage.[32] Doing so would reduce average benefits, since earnings for years presently excluded are inevitably lower than the 35-year average. If, for example, the averaging period were extended from 35 to 38 years—a widely suggested increase—benefits would be reduced by an estimated 3 percent, cutting the long run revenue shortfall by around 12 percent.[33]

Supporters of this proposal argue that most people work more than 35 years, so incorporating additional years would more accurately link benefits to career earnings. Some analysts believe it's unfair that not all contributions to Social Security are considered in determining benefits. Eugene Steuerle pointed out, for example, that according to the current formula, "fifty years of work at [an average of] $35,000 [per year] will yield lower benefits than 35 years at [an average of] $50,000 [per year]." Steuerle argued that lengthening the averaging period would diminish discrimination against people who have worked more years.[34]

Others have argued that lengthening the averaging period would be a mistake, since decreases in benefits would weigh most heavily on those who worked less than 35 years, particularly on women who stayed home to raise children. Their average wage would be depressed by the inclusion of zeros for years they didn't work.[35] Three out of four women but only one out of four men have worked 35 years or less.[36]

Lengthening the averaging period would also hurt the poor more than the rich. According to the benefit formula, a reduction in the average wage would reduce benefits by 90 percent of the wage reduction for a low-income worker but only 15 percent of the wage reduction for a high-income worker. Economists Dean Baker and Mark Weisbrot have calculated that extending the averaging period to 38 years would reduce the benefits of high-income males and females by an average of $191 a year but would cut the benefits of low-income females by an average of $403 a year.[37] They point out that this low-income group, consisting of 2.4 million people, are much more dependent on Social Security than those who are better off, receiving 83 percent of their income from Social Security.[38]

Lengthening the averaging period would cause an across-the-board reduction in benefits, which nine out of ten Americans reject.[39] Nevertheless, the idea is a favorite among politicians.[40]

Increasing the Normal Retirement Age

The normal retirement age—the age at which full Social Security benefits are available—was 65 until 2000, when, as a result of a law passed in 1983, it began a slow increase. It is scheduled to reach 67 by the year 2022.[41] Throughout this period, reduced benefits will be available at age 62 as they are now.[42] A slim majority of the Advisory Council (7 of 13) favored accelerating the increase in the normal retirement age so that it would reach 67 by 2011. These members recommended continuing to raise the retirement age after 2011 in response to increases in longevity.[43] Putting this recommendation into effect would depress benefits by enough to eliminate almost 25 percent of the long-term deficit.[44] As the seven members of the council put it, "The rationale for raising the NRA is that as life expectancy increases, so should the length of the work life."[45] Since Social Security was enacted in 1935, average life expectancy for a person who reaches age 65 has increased by three years for men (77 to 80) and six years for women (78 to 84).[46]

The other six members of the council were concerned about increases already scheduled for the normal retirement age and argued that the effects of those increases should be evaluated before more changes are enacted.[47] They pointed out that just because people live longer doesn't necessarily mean they'll want to work longer or that they'll be able to find jobs. In fact the average retirement age has been falling. These council members worried that raising the age at which people qualify for benefits might disproportionately harm lower-paid and blue-collar workers. "Early retirement may not, in fact, be voluntary for those who are in physically demanding jobs," they said.[48]

This issue arouses strong emotions. Consider, for example, an op-ed piece by *Newsweek* columnist Robert J. Samuelson.[49] He quoted Vice President Al Gore as declaring, "We will reform Social Security the right way. We won't raise the retirement age." Samuelson responded, "It is hard to imagine a more irresponsible promise. . . . Retirees are increasingly healthy and able-bodied." He argued that the retirement age "should go to 68 or perhaps to 70."[50]

Samuelson's article failed to mention that the normal retirement age is already scheduled to go up, something that 50 percent of Americans weren't aware of in 1999, one year before the increase was to begin.[51]

Many proposals recommend increasing the retirement age faster and further than is currently scheduled. A proposal by Senator Daniel Patrick Moynihan would increase it to 67 in 2011 and in stages to age 70 by the year 2073.[52]

A slim majority of the Advisory Council also recommended raising the initial age at which Social Security benefits are available. They favored delaying retirement beyond age 62 because of "improvements in health and longevity and the potential [output] gains to the economy." Approximately one out of four working men retire at age 62, even though doing so lowers their benefits as well as those of their spouses.

What about people unable to work beyond age 62? The council majority noted that "the disability program is specifically geared to meeting the needs of older workers who cannot continue to work due to a disabling condition."[53]

Means-Testing

Why should billionaires like Ross Perot or Bill Gates get Social Security? Why not use some kind of means-testing to deny benefits to retirees whose income or assets fall above a certain cutoff point? Welfare programs such as supplemental security income and Medicaid work like that.

The idea of using means-testing for Social Security achieved more popularity in the 1990s than in any other period in the history of the program, but most economists who have studied the issue oppose it, as did the Advisory Council—unanimously.[54] The council argued that means-testing would discourage young people from saving by sending them the message that "if you are a saver . . . you will be penalized by having your Social Security benefits reduced."[55]

Economists say means-testing would also

- penalize work because working extra hours before retirement could cut workers' benefits;[56]
- be costly to administer because the government would be forced to periodically evaluate retirees' assets, many of which lack a clear market value, and to make sure people don't hide their assets;[57]
- violate the "fundamental political compact that underlies Social Security,"[58] namely, that paying Social Security taxes over a working lifetime earns workers the right to benefits based on their earnings;
- transform Social Security into a welfare program. Public assistance is harder to defend against political attacks than Social Security. Witness the recent termination of the welfare program Aid to Families with Dependent Children;[59]
- erode political support for Social Security among the well-to-do, since higher income workers would pay the same payroll taxes but receive less benefits or no benefits at all.[60]

None of the major proposals to rebalance Social Security includes means-testing.

THE "MONEY'S WORTH" PROBLEM

If you were free to invest your payroll taxes in stocks or bonds instead of handing them over to the Social Security Administration, your return would very likely exceed your Social Security pension. As President George W. Bush put it, "Today young workers who pay into Social Security might as well be saving their money in their mattresses."

The "money's worth" of Social Security, defined as the ratio of pension income received to payroll taxes paid, is low. Experts predict it will drop even lower in the future as a greater percentage of our population reaches retirement age and the number of workers supporting each retiree declines.[61] This, in a nutshell, is the money's worth problem.

Social Security provides more than a retirement pension, however, and to compare the program to an investment portfolio is misleading. It is also a social insurance program, protecting retirees against inflation, disability, and death of a breadwinner. In addition, Social Security redistributes income from high- to low-earning workers. Money's worth calculations focus only on the retirement pension part of the system and ignore these additional benefits.[62] One reason for this narrow focus is that some of the other benefits are not available on the private market. Consequently it is impossible to put a dollar value on them.[63] The true rate of return on Social Security—if it could be measured—would be higher than money's worth calculations suggest.

Nevertheless, many people think it's unfair that our children will receive a smaller pension benefit per dollar of payroll taxes than we do. The Advisory Council, for example, unanimously favored "the objective of improving the money's worth given by Social Security to younger generations."[64]

How could this be done? By enacting policies that increase the rate at which the economy grows. One way to make the nation's income rise faster is to save more and consume less (assuming total spending is maintained by the government). The government could boost national saving and reduce consumption by raising payroll taxes or cutting benefits.[65] Higher national saving would increase the amount of money available to businesses, bringing down the interest cost of borrowing. Lower interest would stimulate firms to increase investment in such assets as factories, equipment, research and development. A growing stock of these assets would boost the productivity of the labor force. If workers produced more goods and services, our nation's income would be higher. As the CBO summarized it, "Increased [national] saving would result in more investment, which in turn would enable the economy to grow at a faster pace."[66]

A faster-growing national income would raise the return our children and grandchildren receive on their payroll taxes. To see why, keep in mind that Social Security is a pay-as-you-go system; that is, the payroll taxes of current workers pay the benefits of current retirees. Suppose we raised payroll taxes or cut benefits.[67] Reduced consumption would augment national saving and generate a faster growth in national income, causing wage income, hence payroll taxes, to increase at a faster pace well into the future. Consequently, our children would receive a better return on their payroll taxes, for although their payroll taxes would have increased because of their higher wage income, the payroll taxes of *their* children would have increased by even more, boosting the amount of money available for their parents' Social Security pensions. The same logic implies an improvement in the money's worth of Social Security for our grandchildren and their progeny. In sum, the money's worth of Social Security for future generations would improve, thanks to the sacrifice imposed on current wage earners and retirees.[68]

The term used for this kind of sacrifice is "advanced funding." The Advisory Council unanimously recommended that we increase the nation's saving by "advance funding for Social Security,"[69] that is, by raising current Social Security taxes or reducing current benefits.

In the first section of this chapter, I examined several ways Social Security revenue could be increased or benefits decreased. Any combination of these could constitute advance funding, which would not only solve the problem of insufficient revenue but could improve the future money's worth of Social Security. The cost of these proposals would be borne by current generations, for their taxes would be raised or their benefits lowered.

Advanced funding is not the only way to increase future national income. We could, instead, raise income taxes on the current generation so that government spending on such future-oriented projects as infrastructure, research, children's health care, or education could be increased.[70] Some people attach a higher priority to these public investments than to increasing national saving.[71] As Aaron and Reischauer put it, "Many of these activities could improve the lives of both current and future generations."[72]

Another approach would be simply to ignore the money's worth problem and resign ourselves to the possibility that the return on Social Security will decline over future generations. Whether or not we should penalize ourselves in order to benefit future generations is a value judgment. Economists agree that with or without advanced funding or additional public investment our children will be richer than we are and their children richer than they are.

CONCLUDING COMMENTS

In this chapter, I've examined several ways we could raise Social Security revenue or cut benefits in order to eliminate the long-run deficit. These changes could also improve the future financial return on Social Security—the so-called money's worth. How one selects from among these proposals is ultimately a subjective judgment. Note, however, that none of them constitutes a fundamental change in Social Security. They do not, as do the two major proposals for restructuring Social Security, involve diverting payroll taxes into the stock market.

The main point of this chapter is that the major problems of Social Security—the long-run deficit and the declining money's worth—could be solved without fundamentally restructuring the system.

Just because the problems of Social Security could be solved without changing its structure doesn't mean that's the way it should be done, however. Restructuring may be a better way. Privatizing Social Security, for example, might come to be preferred by the American people. It, too, is being presented as a way of solving the major problems of Social Security. I examine privatization in the next chapter.

CHAPTER TWO

Should We Privatize Social Security?

No one expected privatization to be a central issue in the 2000 presidential election between George Bush and Al Gore. No one expected it to be an issue at all. Social Security had long been considered the third rail of American politics—"touch it and you're toast." Politicians and economists agreed that no major changes were in the offing. Bush changed all that when he presented his plan to give younger workers the option of investing a portion of their Social Security payroll taxes in personal retirement accounts.[1] Bush made sure privatization would be a major part of the election debate by highlighting it in his acceptance speech at the Republican National Convention. After the election he continued to lobby for privatization. In a speech on February 28, 2002, President Bush once again spelled out his plan to overhaul Social Security:

> Because there will be an expanding number of retirees for Social Security to support in the future, we must apply the power of savings, investing and compound interest to the challenges of Social Security by introducing personal retirement accounts into the system. Americans would own these assets. After all, it is their money. They would see more retirement income, and that's necessary as people live longer lives. And, as importantly, they would be able to pass these accounts on to their children.[2]

Everyone agrees that permitting younger workers to divert a portion of their payroll taxes into personal savings accounts would constitute a fundamental restructuring of our public pension system, but the agreement stops there. Bush's plan was supported by most Republicans and some Democrats including former Senator Daniel Patrick Moynihan (D-NY), Senator Bob Kerrey (D-NE), and Representative Jerrold Nadler (D-NY). Most Democrats opposed it. Al Gore condemned it as "stock market roulette."

Privatization was strongly endorsed by seven out of thirteen members of the Advisory Council on Social Security and just as strongly opposed by the other six. It was recommended by the bipartisan National Commission on Retirement Policy[3] but opposed by the National Commission on Social Security Reform appointed by President Reagan and chaired by Alan Greenspan.[4] A 1994 study by the World Bank argued for privatization, and a 1996 report by the International Monetary Fund opposed it.[5] There was also a split among the experts in the 1999 *Report of an Expert Panel of the National Academy of Social Insurance.*[6]

Supporting Bush's privatization plan are such highly respected economists as Edward Gramlich, chair of the Advisory Council,[7] and Martin Feldstein, chair of the Council of Economic Advisors under President Reagan.[8] Feldstein argued, "Adding individual retirement accounts will only make future retirement incomes more secure."[9]

Opposed to Bush's plan are many equally distinguished economists such as Robert Reischauer and Henry Aaron. They believe that individual retirees are inadequately equipped to deal with the risks of personal retirement accounts as part of the nation's core retirement pension.[10]

The topic of privatization seems to inspire economists, reputedly such a bloodless lot, to exchange barbed rhetoric in ordinarily restrained academic tomes. The dialogue below captures two experts going at each other on the issue of whether contributions to a personal retirement account should be labeled a tax. Listen to John Shoven responding to Henry Aaron:

> He states that I favor plans that raise taxes the most. These statements are simply not accurate. Payments to your own account, even if mandatory, are not taxes. The money is held in your name and will benefit you and/or your beneficiaries. You manage the money and receive quarterly statements about its status. To differentiate this program from a tax increase, simply ask yourself when the government allowed you to designate how you would like your taxes invested for your benefit. The answer, of course, is "never."[11]

Aaron replied:

> I know of no economist who does not regard forced saving schemes as a tax at least in part, because individuals are forced to use their incomes for something that they preferred not to use it for. I also know of no better definition of the word "tax" than "government action to require people to use their income for something that they did not want to use it for." Let us be straightforward.[12]

I see this quibble over definitions as vacuous, but it does give you a sense of how strong are the emotions aroused by the issue of privatization.

One reason evaluating privatization is such a slippery matter is that the debate involves personal value judgments. What's a benefit to one person is a cost to another. Allowing individuals greater freedom to invest their payroll taxes while at the same time reducing our commitment to the poor could be seen as a plus or a minus depending on your values. It may not be an exaggeration to say the debate over privatization is a debate over what kind of society we want for the future. That's why the subject is so emotional. The economist Alan Blinder touched this deeper issue by arguing that Social Security is "one of those precious ties that bind our society together" and that "privatization, whether partial or total, would weaken that tie."[13]

In this chapter, I examine the arguments for and against privatizing Social Security and evaluate the experience of two countries that have privatized their public pension systems: Great Britain and Chile. Finally, I discuss the report of President George W. Bush's commission, which was given the charge of strengthening Social Security through privatization.

WOULD PRIVATIZATION BOOST RETIREMENT INCOME?

Supporters of privatization argue that allowing workers to divert a portion of their payroll taxes into personal retirement accounts would increase their retirement income if the money were invested in a balanced portfolio.

Politicians and columnists routinely compare the average return from stocks to the return on Social Security. Since stocks generally do better, they jump to the conclusion that privatization would generate higher income for retirees.

President George W. Bush has said that the real rate of return on Social Security is "a dismal 2 percent a year."[14] As his economic advisors pointed out, "Over the long term, sound investments in a balanced portfolio of stocks and bonds yield about a 6 percent return after inflation."[15] The same point was made by members of the Advisory Council who endorsed privatization.[16]

Their conclusion? To boost retirement income without raising payroll taxes, divert some of those taxes into personal retirement accounts and give workers the option of investing the funds in private assets.

The logic sounds irresistible. Everyone agrees that in the long run the rate of return is greater on stocks than on Social Security and that holding a balanced portfolio is better than holding only one asset. So why would any rational person quibble?

Perhaps because this conclusion is wrong. Contrary to conventional wisdom, *experts agree that privatizing Social Security is as likely to lower as it is to raise the average income of retirees, even if stocks continue to do well in the future.* Some scholars even conclude that replacing a portion of Social Security benefits with income from personal retirement accounts would shrink average retirement income.

As Henry Aaron put it, "A well-managed Social Security system will generate higher average returns for pensioners than will personal accounts."[17]

Why, when stocks earn a higher return than Social Security, wouldn't privatization boost the income of retirees? There are several reasons.

The Revenue Hole

If payroll taxes were diverted into personal retirement accounts, the Social Security system would be deprived of the money. Diverting 2 percentage points of the payroll tax, for example, would result in a loss to Social Security of trillions of dollars over the next quarter century.[18] But the government has made a commitment to pay a certain level of

Social Security benefits to the retired and those near retirement. So under Bush's plan, the same pot of money is being claimed for two purposes—to be deposited into workers' personal retirement accounts and to pay current retirees' benefits. Thus privatization would create a financial hole, increasing the long-run deficit in Social Security. For several decades, workers would not only have to build up there own retirement accounts but would also have to pay the pensions of older workers who were not part of the new system.[19]

This loss of funds created by the switch to the new system is referred to as the "transition cost." It would fall on only the first few generations who were allowed to divert payroll taxes into personal retirement accounts.

In order to honor President Bush's commitment to pay a certain level of benefits to the retired and near retired, the government would be forced to plug up the drain created by personal retirement accounts. How might this be done? The most obvious solution would be to raise Social Security taxes. But then the return received by the affected generations from a privatized Social Security system would be diminished by the extra cost of higher payroll taxes. In their study of the money's worth of Social Security, economists John Geanakoplos, Olivia Mitchell, and Stephen Zeldes concluded that "the most popular argument in favor of social security privatization . . . that it would increase rates of return for all retirees . . . is false."[20]

Some economists are convinced the transition cost would be so large that it would force the government to renege on its pledge to maintain benefits for the retired and near retired.[21]

RISK

If stocks are such a great investment, why don't we put all our savings in the stock market? The answer is clear. Stocks are risky. Their future value is more uncertain than that of CDs, money market accounts, or Treasury bonds. That's why stocks must offer a higher rate of return: People wouldn't take the risk if they didn't expect a higher return over the long run. When considering the well-being of investors, it makes no sense to look at the rate of return of a portfolio without considering its risk.[22]

Stocks are also riskier than Social Security. Under the current Social Security system, the retired know what their monthly benefit will be. And the rest of us have a pretty good idea, especially now that the Social Security Administration is sending us personal statements. Not so if we were investing part of our payroll taxes in the stock market. Many factors create uncertainty about the income we can expect from a personal retirement account: what stocks we invest in, what happens to the stock market over our working years, the date of our retirement, and whether we take our accumulated savings as a lump sum or use it to buy an annuity. By contrast, under Social Security our retirement income is determined only by our wage history and the benefit formula. Studies show that fluctuations in stock prices and interest rates have extremely small effects on Social Security benefits.[23]

But nothing is risk free, including Social Security. The trust fund could wind up depleted because the economy did badly or because people lived longer than expected. A key difference between the risk associated with the current Social Security system and the risk associated with personal retirement accounts is in who bears the risk. With personal retirement accounts, the risk would be borne largely by the individual. With current Social Security benefits, the risk can be spread over current and future workers and beneficiaries. Social Security's financial emergency of 1983 provides a good example of how Congress spread the risk: it postponed the COLA for six months, speeded up scheduled increases in the payroll tax, instituted a gradual increase in the normal retirement age, and imposed an income tax on the benefits of upper income wage earners.[24]

Some advocates of privatization argue that the risk of Social Security is actually greater than the risk of personal retirement accounts. They distinguish the financial risk from the political risk. For example, members of the Advisory Council who favored privatization believed that "the political risks attached to government benefit promises 20, 30, or 40 years down the road far outweigh the financial risks of a well-diversified portfolio."[25]

We have no crystal ball to predict Social Security benefits or portfolio earnings decades away, but past performance may give us a guide. One measure of the risks to Social Security is the variability in the ratio of monthly benefits to average monthly preretirement wage income. This ratio is referred to as the replacement rate. If your average monthly income before retirement was $4,000 and your monthly Social Security benefit is $1,600, your replacement rate is 40 percent.

Economist Marilyn Moon has studied the variability in Social Security benefits.[26] Her research shows that the stability of replacement rates has been striking. For average earners born between 1919 and 1935 the replacement rate ranged between 43.2 and 40.9 percent. Projected rates for future workers range between 41.5 and 41.7 percent[27] (55.7 to 56.0 percent for low-income workers; 25.6 to 27.5 percent for high-income workers).

This stable relationship between benefits and pre-retirement income is consistent with the promise that Social Security will provide a core of assured retirement income to retirees and their families.

What about replacement rates for personal retirement accounts? In a widely cited study, the economist Gary Burtless simulated the performance of personal retirement accounts invested in the stock market.[28] He found enormous year-to-year variations in the replacement rate for average earners investing their entire payroll tax in a stock market index fund over a 40-year period and converting the savings into an annuity at age 62.[29] The replacement rate fluctuated between 20 percent and more than 100 percent. The average worker who retired in 1969 would have earned a replacement rate of 104 percent, while the rate would have been only 39 percent if this worker had retired six years later.

Replacement rates would have been considerably lower had Burtless considered in his calculations administrative costs associated with privatization such as insurance company fees and costs of fund management and annuitizations, costs that cut into the income from personal retirement accounts. Such an adjustment would not, however, alter his basic finding of large year-to-year fluctuations in the replacement rate.

Burtless didn't examine variations within each year. These fluctuations can also be large. As Aaron and Reischauer have pointed out, "Workers who sold their holdings at the market close on October 19, 1987, would have realized 18 percent less than workers who sold the day before."[30] Even workers who make the same contributions and retire on the same day could have very different pensions due to holding different portfolios.[31]

Many workers would not choose to put all their personal retirement account into a stock market index fund. Instead they might select a mix of stocks and bonds.[32] Though the fluctuation in long-term bonds through changes in inflation and interest rates mimics that of stocks, it is smaller. Bonds also average a lower real return than stocks. Burtless extended his research by performing his simulation for a portfolio consisting of 50 percent stocks and 50 percent bonds. He found the replacement rate to fluctuate between 30 and 70 percent.

Workers could diminish the volatility in the value of their personal retirement accounts by adding short-term securities and money market instruments to their portfolios, but the long-term real return on these assets (adjusting for inflation) has been close to zero.

It's important to note that Burtless did not analyze any of the current privatization plans. Almost no one is recommending that the entire payroll tax go into personal retirement accounts. Partial privatization is being proposed. What Burtless's research demonstrates is that the greater the fraction of the payroll tax diverted into personal retirement accounts, the greater the risk to the wage earner, because the replacement rate associated with retirement accounts fluctuates far more than that associated with Social Security benefits.

The issue of risk has caused many analysts to question the wisdom of privatization proposals. For example, actuary Stephen Kellison and economist Marilyn Moon argued, "Investment safety is more important for the social security program than for most investors, because it is the basic source of retirement income." They question whether Social Security should be exposed to the same kind of risks as personal savings and private pensions.[33]

Administrative Costs

Experts agree that the cost of administering personal retirement accounts would be significantly greater than the cost of administering Social Security. The additional costs would involve sales, advertising, and management fees. Social Security involves none of these expenses because it's mandatory and almost universal.[34]

Believe it or not, Social Security is extremely efficient to administer. As economist Yung-Ping Chen and Social Security actuary Stephen Goss observed in their study of administrative costs, "over 99 percent of all income into the system will be paid out in the form of benefits. No private insurer approaches this level of administrative efficiency."[35] In fact, administrative costs of most private pension plans run to at least 10 to 15 percent of benefits.[36]

Precisely how high the administrative costs of retirement accounts could go depends on how much freedom workers were granted in selecting investments. Usually, the greater the freedom, the greater the cost. The cost could be minimized, for example, if investments were limited to passively managed index funds that did no advertising and had no sales force. But most privatization proposals include no such restrictions, and without them commissions for financial companies would soar. Also, workers and retirees would be the targets of confusing and expensive advertising campaigns.[37]

The economist James Schulz has studied privatization in Britain, where it was instituted in 1986. He observed that administrative expenses have been very high and have shown no tendency to come down. According to the British Institute of Actuaries, administrative costs have resulted in a 10 to 20 percent reduction in the money going into an individual's retirement account.[38]

The bottom line here is that regardless of which privatization plan were adopted, continuing administrative costs would reduce the return on retirement accounts considerably more than they do on Social Security.

Cost of Creating a New Administrative System

Privatization would create still another type of cost. A system would have to be put in place to administer the program.[39] Little discussion has been devoted to this complex issue. As many as 150 million personal retirement accounts and 6.5 million employers could be involved. The administrative challenges and costs of creating such a system would be daunting.[40]

At a minimum, a structure would have to be created to transfer the payroll taxes into personal retirement accounts, allocate these funds to the selected investments, keep records of deposits and earnings, and provide information to employees and the government. Every employer would be involved, since payments to the new accounts would be deducted from payroll taxes. This involvement could be costly, especially for small employers. The interest of workers and employers might clash, workers desiring the freedom to make frequent changes in their investments and employers seeking to hold down costs. The government would have to police the whole process, which would involve regulatory and enforcement costs.[41] All these expenses would shrink the return on retirement accounts.

Think about the administrative questions that would have to be answered:

- To how many investment funds could employees contribute and how often could they move their money?
- How would a company qualify to sell investments to holders of personal retirement accounts?
- Would employers be required to explain investment choices to their workers?
- How would the system ensure that interest and dividends were credited to retirement accounts in a reliable and timely fashion, and how would workers be compensated if something went wrong?
- How would differences between employers' reports, investment firms' reports, and employee's claims be reconciled?
- Would the government's administrative costs be charged to the Social Security Administration?

Robert Ball questioned whether employers would be willing to make more frequent reports than they are now required to do for Social Security. More frequent reporting would add to firms' operating costs and could constitute a major increase in their responsibility.[42]

EARLY ACCESS TO RETIREMENT ACCOUNTS

People often cave in to temptation when it comes to their retirement nest eggs. That was one of the reasons for Social Security in the first place: to force wage earners to save toward their own retirement and to make sure the savings were used for that purpose.

What is the likelihood that the government would prevent workers from spending their personal retirement accounts before they retired? The accounts, after all, would have their names on them and would be, in some sense, their own property. Shouldn't we have control over our own property? people might argue. Suppose a family demanded early access to their personal retirement account due to a medical emergency or college tuition or for living expenses during a spell of unemployment?

The prospect that the government could resist such demands is not promising. Consider the history of Individual Retirement Accounts (IRAs). Initially, early withdrawals were subject to both income tax and a 10 percent penalty, but in 1996 the penalty was removed when the money was used for medical care or health insurance for the unemployed. In 1997, early withdrawals were allowed without penalty for purchasing a first home and for college expenses.[43]

Scholars who study Social Security agree that early access poses a serious problem for privatization. Here are a few examples of expert opinion on this issue:

- The Expert Panel of the National Academy of Social Insurance concluded that "some access to individual accounts before retirement age is likely to be allowed."

- The political scientist Hugh Heclo argued that "the political attraction of selling forced savings with the idea that 'it's your own money'—will make it more difficult in the long run to sustain such nest eggs for retirement."[44]
- Aaron and Reischauer predicted that the government would cave in to pressures to relax restrictions on withdrawing funds from personal retirement accounts. As the restrictions are relaxed, the probability increases that retirement accounts will be cashed in before retirement.[45]

Loss of Social Security Benefits

A personal retirement account would be of little value to the children of a parent who died at 25 or to a person who was disabled at 30. There would be too little money in those individuals' accounts. Yet according to almost all privatization plans, Social Security survivor and disability benefits would be cut.[46] Though reductions in *retirement* benefits would be offset to varying degrees by income from the personal retirement accounts, the same would not be true for survivor and disability benefits. To remain adequately insured, workers would have to buy costly private insurance, which would expose them to high administrative costs and the tendency of private insurers to discriminate against high risk customers. At present, private disability insurance is so costly that few are able to afford it.[47] There's no reason to expect that to change.

The crucial point here—a point I've made before and will make again—is that Social Security consists of more than just a pension; it also insures against loss of income due to the death or disability of a breadwinner. Privatization would reduce this protection.

In the following section I will look more closely at the benefits provided by Social Security in order to evaluate its true rate of return.

PRIVATIZATION AND THE BROADER VALUES OF SOCIAL SECURITY

In my judgment a major source of controversy over Social Security reform is a difference in values between privatizers and anti-privatizers. Advocates of the present system emphasize collective security, helping the less fortunate, and the idea that we're all one family. Supporters of privatization focus on freedom, ownership, and individual responsibility.[48]

Experts agree that comparing the rate of return on Social Security with that of a portfolio is like "comparing apples and oranges."[49] Social Security was never intended to be an investment portfolio. Its goal was to provide social insurance, that is, to cushion income shocks caused by retirement, disability, inflation, low earnings, and the death of a breadwinner. *Rate-of-return calculations are based on retirement income alone,* ignoring the other benefits that Social Security provides. As Hugh Heclo put it, "Rate-of-return calculations deal with future retirement pensions but do not capture all the benefits that people seem to value in the existing Social Security program," including its "social solidarity mission."[50]

It would be impossible to include all the benefits of Social Security in a numerical rate-of-return calculation. How can you put a money's worth number on a social solidarity mission or on maintaining adequate pensions for low income workers? Too bad, then, that it has become conventional wisdom to think of Social Security as a bad deal because the ratio of retirement benefits to payroll taxes is less than the return on an investment portfolio.

Consider the money's worth of Social Security's disability and survivor insurance. Its value is greater than the cash the government pays to the disabled and to the children of deceased breadwinners. The insurance also adds to our peace of mind. Most of us endorse this idea with respect to private insurance. The fact that our premiums are typically less than our cash benefits doesn't lead us to conclude the insurance is a waste of money. Everyone values a good night's sleep. In fact, what could be a better numerical return on collision or fire insurance than zero? Aaron and Reischauer argued that the value of the insurance provided by Social Security and the "sense of security it provides should be added to the actual pension payments in computing the total return to Social Security."[51]

Social Security is also an anti-poverty program. It keeps twice as many people out of poverty as means-tested programs such as Supplemental Security Income (SSI) and Medicaid.[52] There are passionate feelings pro and con about this characteristic of the system. Though no one opposes a safety net, some are indignant that an anti-poverty program should be buried within our public pension system. It's deceptive, they argue, to hide redistribution from the rich to the poor in a benefits formula that people don't know about and don't understand. A program to redistribute income should be out in the open where it can stand on its own.

Five members of the Advisory Council who supported privatization proposed a plan with two tiers. The first protects against poverty by providing a flat benefit. The second consists of personal retirement accounts. Both tiers would be funded by mandatory payroll contributions. These members argued that in their system income redistribution is not "hidden in complex benefit formulae and eligibility criteria but is a straightforward result of moving toward a flat benefit for full-career workers." They go on to say that the anti-poverty element in their proposal will be "more visible and easier to explain to the American people."[53]

Opponents of privatization believe that the first tier of such a system, the flat benefit, would be seen as welfare for the poor because it would offer few benefits to higher earners. The second tier would provide most of the benefits for the wealthy, since they would put more into their retirement accounts than lower income workers. Anti-privatizers are convinced that any welfare component would shrivel under political attack, as did Aid to Families with Dependent Children, if it were not embedded in a system that also provided benefits for middle- and upper-income earners. Wallace Peterson, for example, argued that in such a two-tier system "the solid support that now characterizes Social Security may disappear. A Social Security house half social and half private probably cannot survive."[54]

Many see the income redistribution embedded in Social Security as an integral part of a cherished value system that requires the more fortunate to help the less fortunate. As the six members of the Advisory Council who rejected privatization put it, "Social Security's redistributive benefits formula . . . helps to protect us all against impoverishment without the stigma of a welfare program."[55]

Some scholars argue that privatization would endanger not only redistribution but Social Security as a whole.[56] If we partially privatized Social Security, a portion of the payroll tax would be diverted into personal retirement accounts. The rest would remain in a scaled-back Social Security program. Personal retirement accounts would not redistribute income, because individuals' contributions would stay in their own accounts. In the scaled-back Social Security system, less money would be available for benefits, so somebody's benefits would have to be cut. Under the current system, benefits for low-income workers are already close to or below the poverty line. Presumably they would not be cut much further. It's the higher income workers whose benefits would probably shrink most. Under these circumstances we could hardly expect higher income wage earners to be enthusiastic supporters of Social Security. They might well agitate for more and more privatization.

To summarize: President George W. Bush has declared that the real rate of return on Social Security is "a dismal 2 percent a year."[57] That statement is misleading and incorrect because the rate includes only retirement benefits and excludes protections against disability, death, and inflation. It also ignores the value of Social Security as an anti-poverty program and as "one of those precious ties that bind our society together."[58]

ARGUMENTS IN FAVOR OF PRIVATIZATION

Many people favor privatization because they assume it would boost retirement income. By now I hope I've convinced you that, given transition costs, risks associated with the stock market, and the costs of administering personal retirement accounts, privatization is not as promising as it looks. Still, many distinguished scholars and policy makers favor this kind of reform. Here are some of their reasons.

EVERYONE COULD HOLD STOCKS

More than half the households in the United States hold no stocks, directly or indirectly, so during the 1980s and '90s, when the stock market was making huge gains, they found themselves watching stock investors rake in huge profits while they were left out. Over the long run, stocks have earned more than Social Security pensions. No wonder, then, that it's an appealing idea to give all workers the option of investing some of their payroll taxes in the stock market.

Financial advisors and many economists consider this to be the main argument in favor of privatization. As economists John Geanakoplos, Olivia Mitchell, and Stephen Zeldes put it, "In our view, the fundamental rationale for social security investment in the stock market rests on the existence of people who are currently constrained from holding equities."[59] The same view is expressed in the 1999 *Report of an Expert Panel of the National Academy of Social Insurance:*

> Investment professionals and economic theory both suggest that most people should hold diversified portfolios, including both stocks and bonds. . . . The lack of stock ownership by many households provides one rationale for diversification of Social Security funds into stocks and corporate bonds. . . . Diversification could occur . . . through individual accounts.[60]

In my view, this reasoning is flawed in its generalizing from personal investment strategies to Social Security reform. Everyone agrees that an individual investor would generally do better to hold a balanced portfolio than a single asset. It doesn't follow, however, that diversification would necessarily be a good thing for Social Security. At the risk of being repetitious: An individual's stake in the Social Security system is not a portfolio. It's a social insurance policy that guarantees multiple benefits. Allowing wage earners to divert a fraction of their payroll taxes into stocks would reduce these benefits. Privatizing Social Security would permit more people the freedom to invest in the stock market, allowing some to increase their retirement income, but whether or not they elected to buy stocks, they would incur the costs of privatization discussed in the first section of this chapter.

As I see it, the issue is not whether holding a diversified portfolio is superior to holding a single asset (it is), but whether it's better to give all workers the option of buying stocks or to maintain the benefits provided by Social Security. The answer depends on a value judgment. Which do you prefer? The opportunity to gamble part of your payroll taxes in the stock market or to retain the government's commitment to provide you a prespecified level of Social Security benefits?

In adopting privatization we would be trading in Social Security benefits that are computed and committed years in advance for an income that depends on the gyrations of the stock market. The result would be a heightened uncertainty about our core retirement income. Many agree with the economist Alicia Munnell that "uncertain outcomes may be appropriate for supplementary retirement benefits, but not for the basic guarantee."[61]

Boosting National Saving

Recall that raising payroll taxes now to pay for future benefits would boost national saving, thereby increasing future national income. As a result Social Security would be strengthened.

Supporters of privatization argue that it would be easier for politicians to raise payroll taxes if voters knew the additional revenue was going into their personal retirement accounts. As we have seen, some privatizers reject the notion that requiring people to deposit money in their personal retirement accounts is a form of taxation. They like to call it a "contribution," even though it's not voluntary. Edward Gramlich, chair of the Advisory Council, uses distinct terminologies in his comparison of a payroll tax increase under a privatized system to the same tax increase under the current system: "It is likely that contributions to individual accounts would be a more popular way to raise overall national saving than the widely scorned payroll tax increases."[62]

That increasing national saving is a good thing is rarely questioned.[63] As Gramlich put it, "Prefunding of future benefits [to increase national saving] should be done, somehow or other."[64] An increase in national saving would require an equal reduction in consumption (assuming a full-employment economy). Current generations would tighten their belts in order to improve the standard of living of future generations. Nothing in the discipline of economics can tell us whether it's good or bad to raise current saving at the expense of current consumption in order to improve the future standard of living. Economists are no more able than anyone else to weigh our pain against our grandchildren's pleasure. It's a value judgment.

Keep in mind as you ponder this dilemma that most of the burden of an increase in payroll taxes would fall on lower income workers. The wealthier could maintain their consumption in the face of higher taxes by saving less or selling some of their assets. The poor save little and have few assets. Robert Ball is one of the few economists who has challenged the widely accepted virtue of raising national saving. He asked, "Is it really desirable to force more saving from the lower-paid for the purpose of increasing their cash income in retirement?"[65]

Stimulating Work Effort

Suppose the government increased payroll taxes. Would the reduction in your take-home pay prompt you to change the number of hours you worked? Would you work more or less? Economists say either is a possibility. You could work more because you wanted to maintain your standard of living. Or you could work less because the reward for your labor has declined. Though individual responses would vary, empirical studies suggest that the labor force as a whole would work less in response to a payroll tax increase.

Privatizers argue that under the current system, the payroll tax discourages work because wage earners perceive little or no benefit from the tax; they simply see it as a reduction in the reward for their labor. But if Social Security were privatized, wage earners would be better able to see the link between payroll taxes and benefits because a portion of the tax would be added to their personal retirement accounts. Consequently—or so the argument goes—privatization would motivate the labor force to work more, which would increase the nation's output.[66]

It's true that under the current system most people don't know how their payroll taxes are related to their future benefits. Just ask a non-economist friend how Social Security benefits are computed and observe the puzzled look. (It may help that the Social Security Administration is now sending out statements informing us about our retirement benefits.) In addition, in many instances people pay Social Security taxes and receive no benefits in return. For example, lower earning spouses frequently claim benefits as a spouse, which means that any payroll taxes they may have paid yield zero benefits. Or, if one works more than 35 years, the additional Social Security taxes yield no benefits for the years in which salaries are lower than the 35-year average.

Under privatization there could be a clearer connection between your payroll tax and your private retirement account. But the link between your payroll tax and your retirement income would be even muddier than it is now. No one can predict the ups and downs in the stock market. Even if privatization did tighten the perceived link between taxes and benefits, research findings suggest that the effect on hours worked would be small.[67]

And finally, would it necessarily be a good thing if people were motivated to work more? Many economists seem to think so. Some of you overworked wage earners may think otherwise.

Other Possible Benefits of Privatization

Supporters speculate that privatization would[68]

- restore confidence in Social Security, especially among the young.
- diminish the incentive to evade taxes because people would feel more a part of the system.

- better protect individuals against the political risk of having future benefits cut because the government would be more reluctant to tamper with benefits that stem from personal accounts.

PRIVATIZATION IN THE REST OF THE WORLD

In 1981, Chile scrapped its existing social security system and adopted a two-tier privatization scheme. The first tier protects against poverty by guaranteeing a minimum income to retirees. The second tier requires mandatory payroll contributions to personal retirement accounts. By the 1990s, Chile's experiment appeared so successful that a string of other countries adopted the Chilean model: Mexico, Argentina, Colombia, Peru, Bolivia, El Salvador, Poland, Hungary, and Kazakhstan.[69] In 1986, Great Britain partially privatized its social security program, using a different model.

At present, Great Britain and Chile are the only two countries with a long enough performance record to yield information that is relevant for the United States. In this section, I'll take a look at their experiences with privatization. Keep in mind that both systems are still in the early stages of development. Two decades is not very long in the life of a social insurance system.

Great Britain: A Red Flag for the United States

In 1978, Britain adopted a pension program called the State Earnings-Related Pension Scheme (SERPS), which was much like our Social Security system. Workers paid social security taxes (as did their employers) and thereby became entitled to receive, upon retirement, a pension that was based on their highest 20 years of earnings.[70] In 1986, however, Prime Minister Margaret Thatcher, using arguments almost identical to those of President George W. Bush, persuaded Parliament to adopt a supposedly voluntary privatization plan.[71] Thatcher's political rhetoric was apparently irresistible—higher benefits, lower taxes, more individual control, smaller government pension costs, reliance on highly efficient private institutions. Under the new plan workers were permitted to leave SERPS and switch to private pension plans that gave them considerable freedom over the investment of their payroll taxes. Workers could select employer-sponsored pension plans or personal pensions offered by a variety of approved financial managers.

As it turned out, Thatcher's plan was only nominally voluntary: the government stacked the deck against SERPS by severely cutting benefits and by subsidizing private pensions. Consequently, more than four out of five workers opted out of SERPS.[72]

There was little political outcry in 1986 when Britain dismantled its social security system. Economist Kent Weaver pointed out that a major reason the transition to a privatized system was so easy was that Britain had experienced Social Security for only a few years. He also pointed to Margaret Thatcher's personal crusade against social security and her large majority in the Parliament.[73]

In the United States, advocates of privatization put forth the British system as a model. Thus it was a rude jolt in August 1998 when the *Wall Street Journal,* hardly an enemy of private financial institutions, sounded an alarm about privatization in Britain with an article titled "Social Security Switch in U.K. Is Disastrous; A Caution to the U.S.?" Subheads read, "Many Britons Suffer Losses on 'Personal Pensions,' Insurers Have to Pay Up" and "Tab May Reach $18 Billion."

In discussing the article, the political scientist Max Skidmore asked whether it had changed privatizers' minds. He answered, "No. Their response was to become strangely silent about the British system, but to continue their campaign [to privatize Social Security]."[74]

The economist James Schulz concluded in his study of the British experience that major problems with the system have gone unresolved and that the British are disenchanted with privatization. A recent government review of the situation found that the British have lost faith in the pension system.[75]

Experts lay part of the blame on financial institutions that provided biased and perhaps purposely deceptive information to lure people into purchasing the pension plans they were peddling. David Blake of the University of London found that as many as 90 percent of those who transferred from employer-sponsored plans into personal plans may have been given bad advice.[76] Kent Weaver concluded that in the late 1980s and early 1990s managers of pension funds used misrepresentation and possibly even fraud to lure up to 2 million people to switch from employer-sponsored pensions to personal pensions that provided less generous benefits.[77] The accounting firm KPMG reported that in every case of a worker switching out of an employer sponsored plan, the salesperson had failed to comply with regulations, by not, for example, taking into account the client's attitude toward risk.[78]

The economist Lawrence Thompson, in his study of different public pension regimes, concluded that Britain's experience demonstrates that under privatization there exists the potential for losses caused by incompetent and perhaps dishonest salespeople. He pointed out that several hundred thousand people in Britain were persuaded to make financial decisions that harmed themselves but benefited the salespeople.[79]

The phrase coined for the national scandal was "pension mis-selling." Government investigation revealed that suspect cases ran into the millions. Investigators estimated that the cost of reviews and compensation would be more than $6 billion. Stringent new standards were adopted, and the government launched a $6.6 million advertising campaign warning people about pension mis-selling and urging them to seek compensation if they believed they had been duped.[80]

Could stricter standards have eliminated the problem? Experts don't think so. You can't transform a tiger into a lamb. Salespeople get paid to sell, not to give sound advice. The more pensions they sell, the more commissions they get. As James Schulz pointed out, "even the financial industry admits [that] no amount of rules and regulations can overcome [this] fundamental contradiction."[81]

In fact, the more stringent rules that were put in place have apparently failed to discourage mis-selling. The *Guardian* sent investigators posing as clients to purchase pensions from the Prudential Insurance Company. They found that salespeople were still selling plans that were most profitable for themselves, not best for clients. On the basis of these findings and evidence from other investigations, Maria Scott concluded in an article in the *Observer* that "despite 10 years of financial regulation, something is still rotten at the core of the financial services industry."[82]

In addition to misinformation, wage earners are confronted with a dizzying array of options—an "over complex choice environment," as economists put it.[83] Richard Disney has observed that more than a hundred providers of government-approved personal pensions offer "different investment portfolios, structures of commission charges, payment structures, annuitization strategies, and so on."[84] Schulz detailed some of the complexities of the system:

> People choosing a Personal Pension must select among "endowment," "unit-linked," and "deposit administration" schemes, each with a variety of variants. They can buy from life insurance companies, friendly societies, unit trusts (i.e., mutual funds), building societies, or banks.

> They must choose an "elected retirement date," which, if different from the *actual* date, can result in a significant loss of benefits. They need to understand the key issues related to a pension's "surrender value" and the large potential losses that might result from early termination. They need to be able to calculate and compare among competing products the widely varying administrative costs that are being charged. And they need to choose among the almost infinite kinds of "annuity" options offered at retirement.[85]

How would you like to navigate this minefield with a guide you didn't trust?

And that's not the end of the British worker's travail. There's also the problem of high administrative costs,[86] which have gone unregulated because the government hoped competition would hold them down. According to the British Institute of Actuaries, administrative charges eat up 10 to 20 percent of every dollar that goes into an individual's pension account.[87] Economist Peter Diamond has calculated that for a person who works for 40 years, receives annual wage increases of 2.1 percent, and holds a portfolio that earns 4 percent a year, a 1 percent annual management fee will reduce the value of the worker's personal retirement account by 20 percent.[88]

Surveys indicate that these costs vary enormously from one company to another. A 1996 *Money Management* survey of various plans found that administrative expenses can reduce the projected value of a pension by 8 to 29 percent.[89] Why can't individuals simply shop around to find the cheapest plan? That's practically impossible because the charges are often invisible to the workers. They are imposed in a variety of different ways and are often disguised.[90]

James Schulz pointed out that those hardest hit by administrative costs are low-income workers and those who tend to change jobs frequently, often women and minorities. The reason is that administrative charges are disproportionately deducted during the first couple years of the plan. Since these groups are most likely to stop paying into the plan during this early period, they often wind up carrying away less than they put in.[91]

There is still one more uncertainty faced by British workers under Thatcher's privatization plan. Upon retirement, they are required to convert most of their pension assets into annuities. The value of an annuity depends on factors investors cannot control or predict, such as interest rates and the market value of the pension assets at the time of retirement. As an extreme example, if a person holding a portfolio of stocks had retired immediately after the stock market crash of October 30, 1987, the annuity would be worth 30 percent less than if he or she had retired a week earlier.[92]

Is the British experience relevant for the United States? Scholars who have studied Britain say yes. James Schulz concluded that if the United States privatized Social Security it would encounter the same problems that Britain has, namely, "complexity and confusion, misselling and fraud, high administrative costs, . . . difficulties of knowing what one's future income will be, and a growing feeling of economic insecurity." He asked, "Why would the United States want to take on these problems?"[93]

Kent Weaver concluded that if personal retirement accounts were introduced in the United States, financial institutions would fight tooth and nail over access to the enormous new market for pensions, creating the possibility of bad advice and even fraud by pension fund managers seeking customers. He argued that lawsuits by disgruntled investors in pension funds would blossom, and that administrative costs would be high and camouflaged.[94]

Clearly the British experience raises a red flag for the privatization of Social Security in the United States. The system being proposed by President George W. Bush and most other privatizers is similar to Britain's.[95]

Chile: Poster Child

The privatization of Chile's public pension program has received more attention from the press and policy makers than any other social security reform in the world.

In the 1920s, Chile instituted a standard social security plan. By the 1970s the system was bankrupt.[96] Everyone agreed it had become increasingly inefficient, complicated, and unfair. In 1981, the military government, motivated not only by the failings of the old system but by a desire to shrink the role of the public sector in the economy, abolished the public pension program with one stroke and replaced it with a privately managed system. To make the new regime more appealing, take-home pay was boosted for those who enrolled.[97]

At the same time, hundreds of state-owned firms were sold to the private sector, including banks, public utilities, the national airline, and the country's largest steel mill. After decades of protectionism, Chile was opened up to international competition, which forced local firms to either die or become more productive.

Chile's economic reform program has so far succeeded beyond all expectations. The country has experienced remarkable growth. The profits of firms and the value of assets have soared. From 1981 through 1994, the real rate of return that workers received on their pension assets fluctuated between 3 percent and 31 percent with an average of around 16 percent. Privately managed pension funds grew from $870 million in 1982 to $22.7 billion in 1994.[98]

Under Chile's private pension system, all covered workers—about 75 percent of the labor force—are required to deposit 10 percent of their earnings into savings accounts held by private financial institutions called AFPs (Administradoras de Fondos de Pensiones).[99] These pension management firms are licensed by the government and are strictly controlled.[100] An individual worker can hold an account in only one AFP at a time, but workers are free to switch as often as twice a year.[101] Each AFP is allowed to offer only one pension fund, which is tightly regulated as to the assets it can hold. Disability and life insurance are also provided by the AFP, which purchases this protection from a private insurance company. For this benefit, workers must pay a fee to the AFP, currently around 3.5 percent of their earnings.

The government imposes lower and upper limits on the rate of return that an AFP can pay its members.[102] If an AFP earns more than the maximum, it is required to put the excess in a reserve on behalf of the workers. If the return on its portfolio is insufficient to pay the minimum, it draws on this reserve. If reserves are insufficient, the government liquidates the AFP and makes up the difference.[103]

As a consequence of the restrictions on AFPs, they wind up holding almost identical portfolios. Thus workers are prevented from selecting a mix of assets that reflects their own personal attitudes toward risk. This lack of choice is one characteristic of the Chilean system that would undoubtedly be unpalatable to supporters of privatization in the United States, where a key rationale for personal retirement accounts is that they give people control over the investment of their savings.

Though the AFPs in Chile were highly profitable during the first 15 years the system was in place, the streak of positive to spectacular rates of return may have come to an end. In 1995 and 1998 the real returns were negative, and the average over this four-year period was only a little over 1 percent.[104]

In addition to regulating retirement accounts managed by AFPs, the Chilean government guarantees a minimum retirement income. If the personal retirement account of a worker yields an income below this minimum, the government covers the difference.[105] The cost of providing this minimum pension has been substantial, in some years exceeding 4 percent of GDP.[106] Sebastian Edwards has argued that these government guarantees create an incentive for lower income workers to reduce their contributions by working outside the system since they will still receive the minimum pension.[107] About 50 percent of the workers who belong to the system have failed to contribute to their savings accounts, which shifts the burden of sustaining them in retirement to the rest of society.[108]

The Chilean system is expensive. Peter Diamond was surprised to discover that the cost of running a privatized social security system was so high.[109] One reason for the high cost is that the AFPs spend huge sums on advertising and marketing. In 1994 Chile had almost 3.5 salespeople per thousand participating workers. The same ratio in the United States would yield almost a half million salespeople. By contrast, the United States Social Security Administration has .5 employees per thousand insured workers.[110]

There is evidence that the administrative expenses of Chile's system have increased in recent years. The sales force has grown steadily, rising, for example, from 3,500 in 1990 to 20,000 in 1996.[111] In August of 1997, Jonathan Friedland reported in the *Wall Street Journal* that he had seen workers at a factory in Santiago surrounded by salespeople trying to persuade them to change pension funds and offering them "free toasters, green stamps and sneakers" to sign up.[112] The number of workers who switched AFPs rose from 300,000 in 1990 to 2 million in 1996. Friedland also reported that Chile's pension system was experiencing falling yields, rising costs, and "a burst of unethical practices." Kickbacks to workers who switch pension funds have become common.

Studies find that Chile's administrative expenses are at least 15 percent of benefits, and, according to some researchers, considerably higher.[113] This loss to pensioners is many times greater than the .8 percent of benefits estimated for the U.S. Social Security system. In

Chile, administrative costs are covered at least in part by charging each account a fixed fee, which is constant across all income categories. These costs hurt the poor more than the rich because they constitute a larger fraction of small accounts than large accounts.[114]

Scholars agree it's too soon to tell whether Chile's pension reform can be deemed a success.[115] The high rates of return of earlier decades are expected to decline to more modest rates in the future. Moreover, these returns have been made to appear higher than then they really were since the transition costs (payments owed for work under the old system) were not charged to workers enrolled in the new system but were handled through infusions of general revenue.[116]

Sebastian Edwards's assessment of Chile's reform is representative of expert opinion:

> The Chilean reform program has been a pioneer in the world. It has successfully replaced an inefficient, unfair, insolvent pay-as-you-go system with a (reasonably) well-functioning privately managed system. Until now, the rates of return of the new system, as well as the pensions being paid out, have been very high. This trend, however, is likely to change in the years to come as Chile's rates of return begin to converge toward world levels.[117]

Could the United States adopt a privatization model like Chile's? Most experts are doubtful that the severe restrictions of the Chilean regime would be viable in the United States, where financial institutions are such a powerful political force.[118] Though Chile has permitted only a small number of tightly regulated companies to sell pensions, Henry Aaron argued that "it is naive to believe that members of the U.S. Congress will tolerate the exclusion from 'a piece of the action' of significant banks, insurance companies, brokerage houses, or mutual funds with offices in their districts or states."[119]

REPORT OF PRESIDENT BUSH'S 2001 COMMISSION TO STRENGTHEN SOCIAL SECURITY

On May 2, 2001, President Bush created a commission to strengthen Social Security. In his speech he laid out the principles that must guide the commission:

> First, Social Security reform must preserve the benefits of all current retirees and those nearing retirement.
>
> Second, Social Security reform must return the Social Security system to sound financial footing.
>
> Third, Social Security reform must offer personal savings accounts to younger workers who want them.[120]

The president argued that "personal saving accounts will transform Social Security from a government IOU into personal property . . . that workers will own in their own names and that they can pass along to their children."[121]

The 16-member commission was hand-picked by the White House to be a bipartisan panel consisting entirely of people who favor privatization.[122] It was co-chaired by former Democratic Senator Daniel Patrick Moynihan and Richard Parsons, co–chief operating officer of AOL–Time Warner.

The commission's final report, more than seven months in the making, was released to the public on December 21, 2001. The report appears to have embarrassed President Bush's supporters and thrown red meat to the Democrats. Instead of rallying around a single plan that the president could present to Congress (as Bush's chief economist, Lawrence Lindsey, had promised), the commission presented three proposals, all vague and incomplete.[123]

The proposals differ in that they allow workers to divert a different percent of their payroll taxes from Social Security into personal retirement accounts. In all three plans the enlarged Social Security deficit would be partially filled by cuts in retirement, survivor, and disability benefits. The remaining shortfall would be eliminated, in the words of the commission, by unspecified "temporary transfers from general revenue."[124]

Supporters of personal retirement accounts were disappointed with the commission's report. As Representative Jim Kolbe put it, "Initially we did think the commission would come up with something more comprehensive and a single recommendation."[125] Senator John Breaux joked that the commission was behaving like Congress by coming up with a laundry list of options. "We created them," he said, "so they would not act like Congress."[126] The *Economist* magazine dismissed the report as "dust to dust" and urged President Bush to get on with privatization.[127]

Republicans seemed to see the report as a hot potato. According to the *New York Times,* "Mr. Bush's Republican allies in Congress are saying that the need for benefit cuts makes his plan so explosive that there is no way they would take up a Social Security privatization scheme until after the election next year. They are too afraid of being attacked by the Democrats."[128] A senior GOP congressional aide, referring to the report, told the *Washington Post,* "Any recommendation that would be brought to the Hill this year [2002] would be dead on arrival, because no one is going to allow Democrats to beat Republicans with it in an election year."[129] The chairs of the commission agreed that the report should be shelved for the time being. Co-Chair Richard Parsons said, "We don't expect we are going to pop this report in, and people will then run around immediately and schedule action. We think it will take a good year or so—or maybe more."[130] According to the executive summary, signed by the co-chairs, the commission recommended that its report be discussed for at least a year before any legislative action is taken.[131]

Because the plans are so sketchy, they are easy to describe:

- Plan 1: Workers would have the option of contributing to a personal retirement account 2 of their 6.2 percent payroll tax (about 16 percent of the employer and employee contributions combined). Retirement benefits would be cut by the amount of the contribution plus interest. Survivor and disability benefits would also be reduced for those taking part in the plan. The report provides little detail about the magnitude of these cuts.
- Plan 2: Workers could contribute to a personal retirement account 4 of their 6.2 percent payroll tax up to a certain amount. Benefits would be reduced as in Plan 1. In addition, benefits would be cut for all workers by linking increases to price increases rather than to the faster growing wage increases, as is currently the case. One estimate finds that this rather obscure change could reduce Social Security benefits in 2070 by almost 50 percent relative to the currently scheduled benefits.[132] To make up for some of these cuts, benefits would be raised for low earners and surviving spouses at the expense of high earners.
- Plan 3: If workers contributed 1 percent of their total income to personal retirement accounts, they would be allowed to invest 2.5 percentage points of their payroll taxes into the same account. Benefits would be reduced as in Plan 2, but the retirement age would be raised, thereby causing an additional decline in benefits for all workers.

Do these plans satisfy President Bush's charge to "return the Social Security system to sound financial footing"? The Commission admitted that its proposals would not restore fiscal solvency without transfers from general revenue. It did not specify where in the budget these infusions might come from.

One of the president's main arguments in favor of personal retirement accounts was that they would allow workers to own personal property they could pass along to their children. As he put it, "wealth should not be a privilege of the few."[133] The commission implicitly rejected the president's argument. It proposed requiring that enough of the assets in workers' personal retirement accounts be annuitized to prevent retirees from living in poverty. (An annuity converts a lump sum of assets into an entitlement to specified periodic payments for life.) As the president's commission put it:

> [At retirement,] individuals should have an immediate right to their money only to the extent that they can continue to support themselves. People with personal accounts should, therefore, be required to take at least some of their money as an annuity. . . . Only when it can be reasonably assured that retirees can enjoy retirement outside of poverty will they be allowed to take money from their accounts as lump-sum payments.[134]

Since lower income workers won't have much money in their personal retirement accounts, this proposal would force them to convert most or all of their accounts into annuities.

Could workers have full access to their personal retirement accounts if they had enough other resources to keep them out of poverty? The commission said no. Other wealth would not be taken into account. All workers, no matter how wealthy, would be required to put some fraction of their personal retirement accounts into annuities.[135]

The reaction to the commission's report by those who opposed privatization was severe, even derisive. Nicholas Confessore entitled his article on the report "Commission Impossible."[136] Paul Krugman said:

> Fortunately, the commission that was supposed to propose a detailed plan came to a farcical end. Its final report declared that private accounts would indeed strengthen Social Security, if they were accompanied by sharp benefit cuts and huge financial injections from unspecified sources. Yes, and a jelly doughnut every morning will help you lose weight if you also cut back sharply on other foods and do a lot of exercise.[137]

Economists Henry Aaron, Alicia Munnell, and Peter Orszag said, "The commission documents provide little detail about the size of the traditional benefit reductions involved in the three plans, which is important to understanding their potential effects." They went on, "The apparent failure of the commission to present even a single plan that eliminates the 75-year deficit in Social Security is remarkable."[138]

In an Economic Policy Institute issue brief, Christian Weller argued that the report "shows clearly that the privatization idea is bankrupt." He concluded that "all of the commission's options leave large financing gaps between 2038 and 2075 that will require additional tax increases to fill."[139]

Finally, Robert Greenstein, in a report from the Center on Budget and Policy Priorities, asserted that while the report has "significant weaknesses" it does "serve one important purpose," namely, to "demonstrate the emptiness of rhetoric that pictures individual accounts as a painless way to restore Social Security solvency without making hard choices regarding reductions in Social Security benefits, increases in payroll taxes, or deep cuts or tax increases elsewhere in the budget."[140]

CONCLUDING COMMENTS

President George W. Bush appears determined to privatize Social Security. He has the support of Republicans, some Democrats, and many analysts who study Social Security. Bush has articulated the public's widespread belief that our children will be better off when they retire if they are permitted to invest some of their payroll taxes in the stock market. Since the average income from stocks exceeds the retirement income from Social Security, Bush's proposal sounds like a clear winner.

It would be nice if the issue were as simple as that, but it's not. Stocks earn more than Social Security, but they do so because they're riskier. In addition, the income from personal retirement accounts would be whittled down for several reasons, some of which are rarely mentioned in the public debate:

- Taxes would have to be increased to cover transition costs of switching to personal retirement accounts.
- Charges imposed by private financial institutions to administer the retirement accounts would be significantly higher than the cost of administering Social Security.
- The government would be forced to create new structures to manage the retirement accounts of as many as 150 million workers.
- The government would likely cave in to pressure to allow workers to cash in their accounts to cover emergencies prior to retirement.
- Diverting payroll taxes into personal retirement accounts would almost certainly decrease disability and survivor benefits now provided by Social Security.

There would undoubtedly be winners and losers under the new system. After all, that's the essence of risk. Individual workers' retirement income would depend on the particular portfolios they had chosen and on the date they retired. On the average, though, our children could very well reap less retirement income under privatization than under the present system, even if the stock market performs well.

I'm convinced that these dollars-and-cents considerations are not the real issue in the controversy over privatizing Social Security. The gut issue is ideological. Many citizens resent the paternalistic character of Social Security. They see our retirement system as an authoritarian parent forcing its children to surrender wages in exchange for a meager pension. They're angry they don't control the income they've earned. They see, buried in arcane rules and formulas of social security, a system under which their payroll taxes are siphoned off to take care of their poorer siblings, some of whom were too lazy to work as hard as they did.

People with this outlook have always hated Social Security. In recent years they've grown into a formidable force, thanks to like-minded views in the George W. Bush White House. This faction has benefited from the projection of a long-term revenue shortfall in Social Security. They're trumpeting that shortfall as a crisis requiring fundamental reform.

An opposing faction has a different philosophy. Its members appreciate their authoritarian parent. They're grateful that everyone is being made to save for retirement, since otherwise many would fail to do so. They're inspired by the idea that we take care of each other. Keeping the family together is a high priority for people with these values. They worry that privatization would unravel the family and promote a society where everyone looks after number one.

It may be overly melodramatic to characterize the bitter debate over privatization as a culture war, but I see it that way. Many supporters of Social Security feel that if the privatization camel gets its nose in the tent, the hump cannot be far behind. Present reform plans usually propose putting between a sixth and a third of our payroll taxes into private retirement accounts, but how long would it be before privatizers demanded 100 percent?

However this conflict plays out, it seems certain to me and many others that the outcome will affect the nature of the society our children grow up in.

CHAPTER THREE

Diversifying the Trust Fund

Privatization is not the only fundamental reform being proposed for Social Security. Former President Bill Clinton and others have recommended that the Social Security trustees be permitted to invest the trust fund in a diversified portfolio that includes private securities as well as government bonds. For convenience I'll call this proposal "diversification."

Right now trustees are required by law to invest surplus Social Security revenue in Treasury bonds. Why this restriction? When Social Security was introduced, Congress feared that if the trustees could invest in private securities the government might unduly influence corporate decision making. They also worried that stock prices would be depressed when the trust fund sold stocks. To eliminate these possibilities,

Congress required trustees to hold only a unique type of Treasury bond, one that is risk free and cannot be traded in the market. Under diversification, this restriction would be lifted.

Both privatization and diversification would funnel payroll taxes into stocks and corporate bonds, but the similarity ends there.

Privatization would give workers some control over how the funds in their personal retirement accounts were invested. In retirement, they would receive from these accounts only what their investments had yielded. If the stock market foundered, workers' pension income would shrink.

Under diversification, payroll taxes would continue to flow into the trust fund and be managed by the federal government. Individual workers would have no say as to which private securities were purchased on their behalf by the trustees. Benefits would continue to be defined by law, as they are under the current system. Ups and downs in the stock market would not directly affect benefits. Only long-run trends might make a difference. If the stock market stagnated for many years, the government would be forced to make up the loss to the trust fund. It would, however, have the option of spreading the loss over current and future generations in a variety of ways.[1]

THE BATTLE OVER DIVERSIFICATION

Don't underestimate the potential importance of diversification. It would constitute a fundamental change in our Social Security system. Trustees would wind up managing an unprecedentedly large portfolio of private securities, and thus the federal government would become a major owner of private industry. Not surprisingly, this proposal has been as bitterly debated as privatization. Diversification was praised by the six members of the Advisory Council who rejected personal retirement accounts, and opposed by the seven members who favored privatization. This division reflects a typical split among scholars and policy makers. Those who support diversification, such as Bill Clinton and most Democrats, oppose privatization; those who endorse privatization, such as President George W. Bush and most Republicans, reject diversification.

People on both sides of the divide criticize the present restriction on trust fund investments. Supporters of diversification ask: Wouldn't retirees have more income if the trust fund could be invested in a diversified portfolio instead of low-yield government bonds? After all, part of the revenue earmarked for Social Security beneficiaries comes from the interest on trust fund assets. If the trust fund earned more, Social Security benefits could be financed with lower payroll tax rates.[2]

The magnitudes involved here are enormous. The trust fund is currently projected to grow over the next 25 years from its present value of about $1 trillion to more than $6 trillion and then to decline to zero over the following dozen or so years.[3] As the trust fund grows, so does the potential to increase its income through diversification.

The six members of the Advisory Council who endorsed diversification argued that the government could manage Social Security a lot better if it did not restrict itself to holding only low-yield Treasury bonds. They pointed out that any manager of a private pension fund would be severely criticized for following such an overly conservative investment strategy.[4] These members went on to argue that diversification might be a magic bullet for Social Security, reducing the long-run deficit and improving the money's worth for younger workers. Nevertheless, they were tentative in pushing the proposal and recommended it be carefully studied before any action was taken.[5]

The other seven members of the Advisory Council contended that it was dangerous for the government to become such a large investor in stocks and private bonds. They feared that there would be irresistible pressures to use the funds for political or social purposes, at the expense of retiree's benefits and corporate independence.[6]

These are the arguments that stake out the battleground over diversification.

THE POLITICAL DANGERS OF DIVERSIFICATION

Would it be politically dangerous for the federal government to own a huge slice of the private sector? Opponents of diversification say yes, arguing that the government would become involved in a serious conflict of interest. On the one hand, the government bears the responsibility for regulating business on behalf of the public interest; on the other hand, under diversification the government would manage a portfolio of private securities on behalf of Social Security participants.[7] As members of the Advisory Council put it:

> [Consider] the situation that we would be facing today if the government were the largest investor in tobacco companies. How could it resolve its responsibility to protect the worth of the assets that were the basis of workers' retirement income security while considering the need to regulate the sale of tobacco products in the interest of protecting the public's health?[8]

Note that President Clinton, in his 1999 State of the Union address, recommended that the trust fund be invested in the stock market and in the same speech threatened to sue tobacco companies.[9]

Some fear that under diversification the government would sacrifice the best interest of beneficiaries in order to invest in projects that were politically appealing. For example, the trustees might steer clear of potentially profitable companies that pollute, provide inadequate health insurance, or manufacture guns. Others would support the trustees in avoiding such investments even if they didn't maximize the income of beneficiaries.

Another fear is that the government might interfere in corporate decisions by exercising its stockholder voting power. As diversification opponents point out, if trustees of a pension fund are managing investments on behalf of others—if, that is, they are fiduciaries—then it's their responsibility to make sure the companies whose assets they're holding are doing a good job, which may involve exercising their voting rights as stockholders.[10] Giving the federal government this kind of power is frightening to many.

How serious are the political dangers of diversification? Policy makers and experts are split. Bill Clinton recommended it while Alan Greenspan opposed it. Two legendary scholars who have played major roles in the evolution of Social Security for the past half century are on opposite sides: Robert Ball favors diversification while Robert Myers denounces it as dangerous.[11]

Henry Aaron and Robert Reischauer considered the political dangers and dismissed them. They argued that experience has shown that these worries are overblown.[12] The experience they alluded to was that of a government trust fund that does invest in stocks and corporate bonds, namely the Thrift Savings Plan, a pension plan for government workers.[13] Aaron and Reischauer asserted that this plan has been successfully insulated from politics and has pursued only financial objectives in the management of its portfolio.[14] In defense of diversification, scholars frequently refer to the experience of Francis X. Cavanaugh, who was the executive director of the board responsible for selecting investments for the Thrift Savings Plan from its inception in 1986 until 1994.[15] Cavanaugh encountered no political problems and he saw no reason why the Social Security trust fund should encounter them either.[16]

The International Monetary Fund also favors diversification. It has argued that the trust fund could manage its investments in such a way as to avoid interference from the politicians.[17]

To be doubly safe from politics, many analysts have recommended that trust fund assets be managed by an independent board, a Social Security Reserve Board, which would be modeled after the Federal Reserve Board. Governors of the Fed are appointed by the president, confirmed by the Senate, serve for 14 years, and cannot be removed for political reasons. In addition, some analysts have recommended that the Social Security Reserve Board be limited in its investments to index funds and be prevented from influencing corporations by voting.[18] (Index funds hold shares of all the firms that make up some collection, or "index." Examples are the Standard and Poor's Index or the Dow Jones Index.)

Are you convinced? Read on! There are equally heavy hitters on the other side.

Alan Greenspan has testified that it's "not credible and not possible" to insulate the trustees from politics. He regards diversification as posing "very far-reaching potential dangers for a free American economy and a free American society."[19]

Economist Wallace Peterson is equally passionate. He pointed out that the Roosevelt administration dismissed the idea of the trust fund buying stocks because it could result in the federal government owning a large portion of the private sector—a kind of "stealth socialism." Peterson went on to argue that the temptation to use these investments for political purposes would be irresistible.[20]

Daniel Shaviro, in his study of Social Security reform, argued that diversification would provide the federal government with an additional instrument to give or deny favors to companies.[21] He rejected the idea that the creation of an independent Social Security

Reserve Board would successfully insulate portfolio decisions from politics.

> Perhaps . . . [Congress] would start by barring investments in tobacco companies and gun manufacturers. Then, mirroring what has happened in state-run funds and those in other countries, Congress might start mandating, say, investment in low-income housing, local infrastructure, or companies that promise to build manufacturing plants in Rust Belt states that hold key presidential primaries. Perhaps, as happened recently in Texas with Disney stock, complaints about the morality of recent film releases . . . would lead to hasty dumping of millions of shares.[22]

The *1999 Report of an Expert Panel of the National Academy of Social Insurance* acknowledged the political risks of diversification, concluding that even with a setup similar to the Thrift Savings Plan there would be political pressure on investment choices and inappropriate influence on corporate decisions. Nevertheless, the panel was divided on this issue, with some of the members concluding that to diversify the portfolio would be worth the political risks.[23]

Generalizing from the Thrift Saving Plan to Social Security is questionable. Under that plan, retirement assets are held in the form of personal accounts. Politicians may be less likely to meddle with pension plans in which the investors have a personal connection with their accounts.[24]

In order to evaluate the dangers of diversification, we can take a look at state and local pension plans that are invested in stocks and corporate bonds. To what extent has the investment of these funds been vulnerable to political pressure? The evidence shows that politics has often overridden the financial interests of pensioners. Eighteen states have statutes requiring that their pension funds be invested in assets that promote local industry.[25] Here are some examples of state pension funds that have incurred losses due to investments based on political considerations:

- In the 1970s the New York State pension fund purchased New York City bonds in order to protect the city from insolvency. Such an investment was hardly likely to earn a competitive return.[26]
- Pennsylvania's pension fund was invested in Volkswagen to induce the corporation to locate in the state. The plant closed some years later, and the loan was not repaid.[27]
- The Kansas pension fund suffered huge losses as a result of investing heavily in local businesses.[28]
- The New Jersey pension fund dumped all assets that were linked to South Africa and lost between a third and a half million dollars in brokerage fees and depressed stock prices.[29]
- Connecticut's pension fund lost $25 million trying to prevent Colt Industries from going bankrupt.[30]

If you feel that the only legitimate objective of a pension fund is to maximize the income of retirees, you may find this record discouraging. Political pressures would almost certainly be applied to the Social Security trustees were they permitted to invest in private securities. Consider this exchange, which occurred during deliberations of the Advisory Council:

> [Council member] Edith Fierst asked the council members representing organized labor, "How would your people feel about a fund . . . investing in non-union, anti-union establishments?" Gloria Johnson from the AFL-CIO replied, "I think it would create some concerns, great concerns." [Council member] Carolyn Weaver sought clarification of the point by asking if organized labor would have a problem

> with passive investment policies through an index fund, for example, the "stocks listed in the S & P 500." . . . Gerald Shea from the AFL-CIO clarified: "I think I . . . [would respond] positively as long as it was buy American and build union."[31]

Nevertheless, trustees might be insulated against political pressure if they were restricted to index funds and prohibited from cherry-picking among individual stocks. This prohibition is widely recommended by scholars.[32] Aaron and Reischauer, for example, argued that the trust fund should be permitted to invest only in passive funds that represent a broad collection of industries.[33]

Would such a restriction be feasible? The issue is contentious. Peter Diamond shares the optimism of Aaron and Reischauer, observing, "Politicians often like having their hands tied: 'Sorry, I cannot do anything about that.'" He goes on to argue, "There are no guarantees, but it seems to me that all of corporate America would be backing that firewall against individual stock-picking, once it was up."[34]

By contrast, Sylvester Schieber and John Shoven, along with five members of the Advisory Council, argued that any type of firewall was unlikely to hold, pointing to the experiences of state and local pension funds as well as public funds in other countries.[35]

As an example, Schieber and Shoven pointed to Canada. Canadian legislation permitted trustees to invest its trust fund in private markets beginning in early 1999. Trustees were limited to index funds for the first three years. The chair, Gail Cook-Bennett, has said that it's not possible to continue such a restrictive strategy and that after three years the board will recommend "that we go active in the domestic market."[36]

Even if trustees could be limited to index funds, there would still be pressure to select certain funds and not others. Theodore Angelis has pointed out that a great many funds refuse to invest in the assets of industries that are socially unpopular, such as tobacco and alcohol. He goes on to say that investing in socially conscious industries and companies has increased by 85 percent since 1995.[37]

The trend was reflected in a position adopted by the Clinton administration that pension funds be required to invest a portion of their revenue in "socially responsible" projects. Such a requirement, while clearly attractive to those who wish to reward corporations for behaving responsibly (however "responsibly" might be defined), may not be consistent with maximizing the income of pensioners.[38]

EISNER'S MAGIC BULLET

Consider once again the rationale for diversification. The trust fund is currently restricted to a special Treasury bond (one that does not fluctuate in value) that is expected to earn only 2.8 percent over inflation. The rate of return on a diversified portfolio averages 6 to 7 percent over inflation.[39] If the trust fund included higher yielding private securities, Social Security revenue would be augmented with no increase in payroll tax rates. Consequently, the money's worth of Social Security would be improved: more benefits from the same payroll taxes. In addition, the long-run deficit would be diminished. But as we have seen, many analysts fear that diversification would concentrate too much power in the hands of the federal government.

Could we have our cake and eat it too? The late Robert Eisner, past president of the American Economic Association, believed that we could. He argued that Congress could simply authorize a higher rate of return on the Treasury bonds held by the trust fund.

Here was Eisner's reasoning: If the Treasury could not borrow from the Social Security Trust Fund, it would be forced to borrow from the private sector. Whenever the Treasury bids funds away from the private sector, businesses—deprived of that money—cut back on investment spending. Thus trust fund surpluses indirectly boost private investment and should receive an appropriate rate of return for doing so. That rate would be approximated by the average return on a diversified portfolio.[40]

Suppose Congress did decree a higher rate of return on the Treasury bonds in the trust fund. The effect would be to increase the indebtedness of the Treasury to Social Security, reflecting an increase in the value of the trust fund. Eisner acknowledged that such a decree would be nothing more than an "accounting maneuver," increasing the obligation of one arm of the government to another,[41] but he believed that future politicians would honor the obligations of the Treasury to Social Security.

Eisner also recommended boosting the value of the trust fund by crediting it with income tax revenue. His rationale was that Americans currently pay income taxes on that portion of their income that goes to Social Security in the form of payroll taxes. That portion of the income tax is actually a "tax on a tax" and should be credited to the trust fund.[42]

Eisner estimated that enacting his measures would raise enough revenue to eliminate Social Security's long-run deficit.

It's clear to me that Eisner's goal was to legitimate the use of income tax revenue to fund Social Security. That is, in addition to payroll taxes, he wanted to use taxes on non-labor income—such as profits, capital gains, dividends and interest—to pay benefits. Under his plan the money's worth of Social Security could be increased. That is, the same payroll taxes could pay more benefits, thanks to an infusion of general revenue.

How do experts evaluate Eisner's idea? Political scientist Max Skidmore was enthusiastic, referring to Eisner's plan as "an ingenious solution" to the problems of Social Security.[43] Daniel Shaviro argued that Eisner's proposal could buttress the commitment to beneficiaries if people really treated the assets of the trust fund as an obligation of the government to Social Security. He went on to say that Eisner's plan could result in income taxes being used to pay benefits instead of payroll taxes.[44] Henry Aaron and Robert Reischauer support Eisner's recommendation, noting that the use of income taxes to finance social insurance is common around the world. They contend that reducing the long-run deficit in Social Security is an obligation of the entire nation and not just workers, because that liability is a result of the generous benefits paid to pensioners in the early years of Social Security. In addition, they argue that using general revenue to pay benefits is justified because Social Security is also an anti-poverty program. If it were cut back, welfare payments to the elderly would have to increase, and welfare is financed by income taxes.[45]

The Advisory Council overwhelmingly opposed Eisner's proposal that Social Security use income taxes in addition to payroll taxes.[46] The council was concerned that Social Security could get caught up in the annual dogfight over the budget. Benefits might be cut if other expenditures were more popular or more pressing that year. If politicians took to adjusting benefits on a yearly basis, Social Security would be radically changed. It has always been a long-run program, one in which people pay Social Security taxes today for benefits that may not be received for decades.[47]

The council's other worry was that the "fiscal discipline" of Social Security could erode if income taxes were used to pay benefits. As it is now, with the payroll tax as the only tax that can be used to pay benefits,[48] benefits can increase only if payroll taxes increase.

The council didn't mention a third concern. Franklin Roosevelt articulated the social insurance rationale for Social Security by asserting that payroll taxes "give the contributors a legal, moral and political right to collect their pensions."[49] Supplementing payroll taxes with income taxes could weaken the perception that benefits are an earned right.[50]

Eisner's proposal is supported by some analysts because they prefer the progressive income tax to the regressive payroll tax.[51] (A progressive tax is one in which the individual's tax rate increases as income increases. With a regressive tax, the tax rate falls as income rises.) Analysts also point out that the wage base that feeds Social Security has been eroding and is expected to decline further over the next several decades. Less and less income is being derived from wages and more from rent, interest, and profits.[52] As a result, some economists argue that the payroll tax, based on wages only, should be supplemented with a tax on non-labor income.[53]

What is the current status of Eisner's recommendation? To my knowledge, his proposals have not shown up in any of the detailed reform plans formulated by scholars and policy makers,[54] but his general suggestion that we increase the obligation of the Treasury to Social Security is very much alive. In fact, it has been espoused by some of our leading politicians.

In his 1999 State of the Union address, Bill Clinton proposed that 60 percent of the budget surpluses projected over the next 15 years be credited to the Social Security trust fund.[55] Legislators on both sides of the aisle cheered.

What was the exact significance of Clinton's suggestion? Even the knowledgeable journalists on the TV program "Washington Week in Review" seemed stumped. It looked to them as if the same money were being used twice, for if a budget surplus retires the public debt, how can the same money be deposited in the trust fund? The answer is that the surplus is not actually being deposited in the trust fund. The only thing you can do with a budget surplus is buy down the public debt. What Clinton was suggesting was that we increase the Treasury's obligation to Social Security by an amount equal to 60 percent of the budget surpluses. Like Eisner, Clinton was recommending that we increase the value of the trust fund by giving it an accounting credit.

Clinton is not the only political leader to make a proposal similar to Eisner's. George W. Bush, in his year 2000 stump speech, said, "I want to take one half of the surplus and dedicate it to Social Security."[56] Former Vice President Al Gore promised he would credit to the trust fund the interest saved by reducing the public debt. While these proposed credits to the trust fund differ in magnitude, they are all, like Eisner's proposed credits, accounting maneuvers that increase the obligation of the Treasury to Social Security.

How do these Eisner-type proposals differ from diversification? Both have the goal of enriching Social Security. Under diversification, the trust fund would be invested in higher yielding private securities in addition to lower yielding Treasury bonds. Under Eisner's proposal, the trust fund would simply be given an accounting credit—a promise by the Treasury to provide more money to Social Security. Under both plans the revenue gain would be matched by losses in the non–Social Security sector. Under Eisner's plan, the losers would likely be taxpayers whose income taxes would increase in order to supplement payroll taxes.

Under diversification, the losers would be private-sector investors. Consider: Excess payroll taxes go to the Treasury, which—given a surplus in the overall budget—uses these funds to retire Treasury bonds held by the public. Under diversification, trustees would use some of the excess payroll taxes to purchase private securities instead of Treasury bonds, thus depriving the Treasury of that revenue. As a consequence, the Treasury would reduce its purchases of government bonds from the public. So under diversification the public would hold more Treasury bonds and fewer private securities, while the Social Security Trust Fund would hold more private securities and fewer Treasury bonds. (The same reasoning holds if the federal government were running a budget deficit.[57]) By bidding higher earning private securities away from the public, Social Security would earn more revenue in the form of dividends and interest. Private sector investors would be saddled with lower earning assets.[58] This would be the hidden tax entailed by diversification. (Of course the trust fund is also incurring more risk while bestowing less on the non–Social Security public.)

PRIVATIZATION VERSUS DIVERSIFICATION, A SUMMARY

Freedom Entails Risk

If Social Security were privatized, young workers would have more freedom to select their investments, but they would bear more financial risk than under the current system. A bad turn in the financial markets would shrink their retirement income.

Under diversification, wage earners would have no control over the securities purchased on their behalf, but neither would their Social Security benefits be directly affected by the financial markets. Benefits would be determined by law, as they are now. In the event of a long run downturn in stock prices, the government could spread the loss by reducing benefits or increasing taxes across several generations.[59]

When it comes to political risk, however, privatization may have an advantage over diversification. The government is less likely to meddle with personal retirement accounts than with assets in the trust fund.

Disability and Survivor Benefits

Under privatization, Social Security would lose money because payroll taxes would be diverted into personal retirement accounts.

Consequently, workers could expect their disability and survivor benefits to be reduced.

Under diversification, Social Security payroll taxes would continue to flow into the trust fund. The trustees would simply have more freedom to invest them. Consequently, there's no reason to expect that disability and survivor beneficiaries would suffer.

Cashing In Early

Under privatization, workers would see their retirement accounts as their own personal property. If the past is any guide, they would pressure the government to make these funds available to them before retirement in cases of emergency, and the government would cave in. As a result the need for public assistance to the elderly would probably increase.

Early cashing in could not occur under diversification because all Social Security assets would be managed by the federal government.

Redistribution

One effect of the Social Security benefits formula is to redistribute income from the rich to the poor. This redistribution would be unaffected by diversification.

Privatization, however, would diminish the anti-poverty effects of Social Security because personal retirement accounts do not redistribute income.

National Saving

If the goal is to boost future national income by increasing national saving, then privatization would appear to have an advantage over diversification. Wage earners would likely be less resistant to higher payroll taxes if the taxes went into their own personal retirement accounts than into a general pool.

Hours Worked

Privatization might encourage people to work more hours than they do under the current system because they could more easily see the relationship between payroll taxes and retirement benefits.

There's no reason to expect the link between taxes and benefits to be any more transparent under diversification than it is now.

Costs of Setting Up a New Administrative System

Under privatization, businesses and government would have to bear the additional costs of setting up a system to manage the personal retirement accounts and the investments of up to 150 million workers.

Diversification would not entail such costs, since all Social Security assets would remain in a central pool, managed by the trust fund.

Administrative Costs

Inevitably, privatization would involve significantly greater continuing administrative costs than diversification.[60]

Political Danger

Under diversification the federal government would own a huge slice of the private sector. In the minds of many, this would increase the danger that the government could unduly influence corporate decision making. In addition, the government would be caught in a conflict of interest, between maximizing earnings on behalf of beneficiaries and investing in projects that promote the general welfare.

Privatizing Social Security would not entail these risks.

A FINAL THOUGHT: WOULD REFORM IMPEDE MONETARY POLICY?

America's first line of defense against both unemployment and inflation is monetary policy, which is conducted by the Federal Reserve System, currently chaired by Alan Greenspan. When unemployment threatens, the Fed lowers interest rates on government securities, reducing the cost of borrowing. This stimulates spending, thus boosting output and employment. When inflation appears on the horizon, the Fed pushes interest rates up, discouraging spending and dampening the upward pressure on prices. The Fed controls interest rates mainly by buying or selling Treasury securities.

Imagine now that Social Security were restructured either by privatization or diversification. As a result, public pensions would become more dependent on the value of private securities, which in turn is affected by monetary policy. For example, if the interest rate on Treasury securities rose, people would be attracted by their higher return and switch funds into Treasuries from stocks and corporate bonds, thus driving down the prices of these private assets.

How would monetary policy be affected if Alan Greenspan had to worry about Social Security in addition to inflation and unemployment? Greenspan is opposed to the federal government investing in private securities, but he doesn't mention any threat to the freedom of monetary policy.[61] Theodore Angelis does mention this worry:

> There are a host of . . . federal decisions that will become more complex as large sums of public money move into the equities markets. The decisions of the Federal Reserve Board may gain more attention and criticism as each interest rate change affects Social Security funding.[62]

The Fed is not supposed to concern itself with stocks and corporate bond prices. In so far as it did feel responsible for the value of private assets, its primary mission would be hampered.

The possible impact of privatization or diversification on monetary policy has been, to my knowledge, unexamined by those who study Social Security reform. Is it a serious problem? If so, would it be worse under privatization or under diversification? We don't know. The question has barely been asked.

CHAPTER FOUR

Questions and Answers

If you've stuck with me this long, you've become somewhat of an expert on Social Security reform. In fact you probably know more than most of your friends. What if they decided to quiz you? How would you respond? To help you prepare for such an encounter, I've written a sort of a crib sheet: questions you're liable to be asked and answers you might give.

Q: How bad is the situation with Social Security? Is it really going bankrupt?

A: Bankruptcy is not a threat, but Social Security *will* need more revenue over the next several decades if retirees are going to get the benefits they've been promised. Experts agree that the changes would be minor and could be carried out in a series of small steps. Fundamental restructuring is not essential.

Q: Then why am I always hearing that Social Security is going broke?

A: Some of the scare mongers have their own agendas. They'd like to see Social Security restructured, and they think predicted shortfalls provide the perfect opportunity to push for it. For example, many people resent having the government manage their retirement savings. They'd rather invest the money on their own, as they could under privatization. And financial institutions would be delighted to see Social Security replaced with personal retirement accounts. They could earn millions in fees.

Q: Why not let people choose whether they want to participate in Social Security? Wouldn't that make everybody happy?

A: Probably not. Under Social Security the rich subsidize the poor. If the system were voluntary, the well-to-do would probably drop out. Social Security would become a program for the poor alone, and that might very well kill it. One reason Social Security is still alive and kicking after two thirds of a century is that everyone is forced to participate and everyone gets benefits.

Q: How much more revenue is Social Security going to need?

A: Experts estimate that if the payroll tax rate were increased right now by about 1 percentage point on both workers and employers, scheduled benefits could be paid over the next 75 years. But no one is recommending that we raise the money that way.

Q: What *are* they recommending?

A: Assuming we want to keep the system more or less as it is, we could

- make Social Security universal by bringing in newly hired state and local government workers;
- tax Social Security benefits the same way we tax private pensions;
- trim scheduled benefit increases for the wealthy.

Those are the least controversial proposals. Others would cause more of a stir:

- increase the retirement age;
- reduce cost-of-living adjustments;
- eliminate the cap on wages that are subject to the payroll tax;
- increase the number of years used to calculate the lifetime average used in the benefits formula.

Q: President Bush said the rate of return on Social Security was so dismal we might as well put our money in our mattresses. Is that true?

A: Bush was looking at retirement benefits only, but Social Security provides a lot more than retirement benefits: disability insurance, survivor benefits, protection against inflation, protection against outliving your assets. These benefits are never included when people compute the rate of return on Social Security, and it's not clear how they could be.

Q: What about Bush's proposal to privatize Social Security? Couldn't we earn a better return on our payroll taxes if we put some of them in private securities?

A: There would be gainers and losers, but experts agree that even if the stock market does well over the next century, the retirement income of the average worker would not increase under privatization and might well decrease. The additional costs of privatization would whittle down the rate of return on personal retirement accounts:

- Social Security would lose the revenue that was diverted into personal retirement accounts, so taxes would have to be increased to honor the commitment to workers who are retired now or will retire soon;

- Setting up personal retirement accounts for up to 150 million workers would impose new costs on both government and employers;
- Personal retirement accounts would be more expensive to administer than Social Security;
- The non-retirement income provided by the current system (e.g., disability, survivor benefits) would likely be reduced under privatization.

Q: What, then, are the arguments in favor of privatization?
A: Among them:

- Creating personal retirement accounts would give workers some options as to how their payroll taxes were invested;
- Privatization would permit lower income workers to put money into the stock market and allow them to invest in the growth of the economy;
- Personal retirement accounts don't redistribute income, a feature that is considered a plus by people who resent the hidden antipoverty component of Social Security;
- The government might be less likely to tamper with public pensions if workers had personal retirement accounts.

Q: What about Chile? Hasn't it privatized its social security program?
A: It has, and the program has done well in the two decades it has been in effect. But workers in Chile have almost no options as to the mix of assets they hold. Only a small number of tightly regulated companies are permitted to sell pensions. It's unlikely that our workers or our financial institutions would tolerate such tight constraints.

Q: Have other countries privatized?

A: Many, but the only one with a track record is Britain. In 1986, Britain adopted a system similar to the one currently being proposed by Bush. Reports indicate that Britain's experience has been disastrous. Private financial institutions have provided biased and deceptive information, many retirees have suffered losses, and there are numerous lawsuits. Experts doubt there's a remedy for Britain's problems.

Q: What about Bill Clinton's recommendation that the Social Security trustees be allowed to invest the trust fund in private securities?
A: The trust fund would probably earn more income that way, given that private securities average a higher return than Treasury bonds. Plus the risk could be spread out over the whole system so individual workers wouldn't bear the whole brunt of a downturn in the stock market.

Q: So is diversification a good deal?
A: It's just as controversial as privatization. The main argument against it is that the federal government would wind up owning a huge piece of private industry and might interfere with corporate decision making. And the government would inevitably be involved in a conflict of interest, since the corporations that yield the highest return to their investors are not necessarily the ones that promote the general welfare.

Q: Are those serious problems?
A: Experts are split down the middle, heavy hitters on both sides.

Q: Are there any other reform plans?
A: Economist Robert Eisner suggested that Congress simply decree a higher rate of interest on the Treasury bonds in the trust fund.

Q: Where would the money come from?

A: Probably from income taxes. Eisner didn't believe Social Security should be funded by payroll taxes alone.

Q: What do experts think of that?

A: They're divided, of course. Those opposed argue that using income taxes to pay benefits could

- entangle Social Security in the annual budget fight;
- undermine Social Security as an earned right;
- weaken the fiscal discipline of Social Security.

But those that support it note that it would

- move away from the regressive payroll tax as the sole revenue source for Social Security;
- give Social Security some grounding other than the wage base, which is shrinking.

Q: What do politicians think?

A: Leaders of both parties agree that we should broaden the base of Social Security beyond the payroll tax. Clinton, Gore, and Bush have all recommended that Congress credit the trust fund either with budget surpluses or with interest saved as we retire the public debt. All these proposals would open the door between the trust fund and general revenue. We would end up using income taxes to pay Social Security benefits. The result would bolster Social Security but not fundamentally restructure it, as would privatization or diversification.

NOTES

INTRODUCTION

1. See the *Status of the Social Security and Medicare Programs: A Summary of the 2001 Reports,* by the Social Security and Medicare Boards of Trustees, March 19, 2002.
2. *Social Security: A Primer,* Congressional Budget Office, September 2001, chapter 2, p. 12, fn. 2.
3. "A Framework for Considering Social Security Reform," by Michael J. Boskin, in *Framing the Social Security Debate,* edited by R. D. Arnold, M. J. Graetz, and A. H. Munnell, p. 30.
4. See "Bridging the Centuries," by Robert M. Ball with Thomas N. Bethell, in *Social Security in the 21st Century,* edited by E. R. Kingson and J. H. Schulz, p. 277.
5. See "Are Social Security Benefits Too High or Too Low?" by Marilyn Moon, in *Social Security in the 21st Century,* edited by E. R. Kingson and J. H. Schulz, p. 66, Table 4.2. Also, 60 percent of retirees receive more than 60 percent of their income from Social Security.
6. *Is it Time to Reform Social Security?* by Edward M. Gramlich, p. 18.
7. For Roosevelt's statement, see *Funding Social Security,* by Laurence S. Seidman, pp. 153–154.
8. *America's Welfare State: From Roosevelt to Reagan,* by Edward Berkowitz, p. 91.
9. Quoted in *Funding Social Security,* by Laurence S. Seidman, p. 154.

10. "Bridging the Centuries," by Robert M. Ball with Thomas N. Bethell, in *Social Security in the 21st Century,* edited by E. R. Kingson and J. H. Schulz, pp. 275–278.
11. See *Basic Facts,* by the Social Security Administration, Publication No. 05–10080, January 2001, pp. 1–2, and *Social Security: A Primer,* Congressional Budget Office, September 2001, chapter 2, p. 4.
12. "Bridging the Centuries," by Robert M. Ball with Thomas N. Bethell, in *Social Security in the 21st Century,* edited by E. R. Kingson and J. H. Schulz, pp. 277–278.
13. See the *Status of the Social Security and Medicare Programs: A Summary of the 2001 Reports,* by the Social Security and Medicare Boards of Trustees, March 19, 2001.
14. Ibid.
15. *The Economic and Budget Outlook: Fiscal Years 1998–2007,* Congress of the United States, Congressional Budget Office, January 1997, and *The Economic and Budget Outlook: An Update,* Congress of the United States, Congressional Budget Office, July 1, 1999.
16. The most recent figure is 1.86 percentage points. This estimate ignores the long-run deficit in the Hospital Insurance portion of Medicare, which is also financed from a payroll tax. Including Hospital Insurance, the 75-year deficit would require a payroll tax increase now of 2.85 percentage points. For these estimates, see *Status of the Social Security and Medicare Programs: A Summary of the 2001 Reports,* by the Social Security and Medicare Boards of Trustees, March 19, 2001, available at www.ssa.gov/OACT/TRSUM/trsummary.html.
17. See *Deficit Hysteria,* by A. Benavie, p. 89.
18. There are actually four separate trust funds for Social Security and Medicare. For our purposes, the first three can be combined into one, which I will call "the Social Security trust fund." The Old-Age and Survivors Insurance Trust Fund (OASI) pays retirement and survivor benefits. The Disability Insurance Trust Fund (DI) pays disability benefits. These two are jointly referred to as the OASDI Trust Fund. Within Medicare, the Hospital Insurance Trust Fund (HI) pays for hospital and related care. The OASDI and HI currently receive the vast majority of their revenue from payroll taxes that are earmarked for these purposes. The Supplementary Medical Insurance Trust Fund (SMI), which pays for physician and outpatient services, doesn't receive any payroll taxes. Unlike OASDI and HI, the SMI Trust Fund never runs a deficit because it is funded by separate fees and draws on general revenue in case of a

shortfall. See the *Status of the Social Security and Medicare Programs: A Summary of the 2001 Reports,* by the Social Security and Medicare Boards of Trustees, March 19, 2002.

19. *The Truth about the National Debt,* by Francis X. Cavanaugh, p. 98.
20. *Is Social Security Broke?* by Barbara Bergmann, p. 82.
21. *Will America Grow Up before It Grows Old?* by Peter G. Peterson, p. 31.
22. See the *Status of the Social Security and Medicare Programs: A Summary of the 1999 Annual Reports,* by the Social Security and Medicare Boards of Trustees, March 31, 1999. These estimates include the total Medicare payments, that is, both Health Insurance (HI) and Supplementary Medical Insurance (SMI). The 2001 report does not include these estimates.
23. This assumes that real income per worker (that is, productivity) will increase, on the average, by only about 1 percent a year. Productivity has never increased that slowly. According to the CBO, trend growth in productivity before 1973 was 2.75 percent a year; from 1973 to 1995 it was 1.5 percent a year, and in the past five years it has been 2.3 percent a year. See *The Budget and Economic Outlook: Fiscal Years 2001–2010,* appendix A, January 2000, by the CBO. Were we to use 2 percent—which is the current assumption of the CBO—the average income per worker would double by around 2035. See *Social Security: A Primer,* Congressional Budget Office, September 2001, chapter 3, p. 7.
24. See *Countdown to Reform,* by Henry Aaron and Robert Reischauer, pp. 59–60, *Is Social Security Broke?* by Barbara Bergmann, p. 96, or *Social Security: A Primer,* September 2001, chapter 1, p. 7, by the CBO.
25. See, for example, *Will America Grow Up before It Grows Old?* by Peter Peterson, p. 40. In the 1994 UFO survey by the Third Millennium, people were asked in two separate questions to evaluate the probability (1) of seeing a UFO and (2) of receiving Social Security benefits when they reach retirement age. Journalists incorrectly compared these probabilities. In 1997, the Employee Benefit Research Institute asked people directly to compare the two probabilities. Respondents sided with Social Security 71 percent to 26 percent. Even among those under 33, the margin was 2 to 1. For these data, see "Myths and Misunderstandings about Public Opinion toward Social Security," by Lawrence R. Jacobs and Robert Y. Shapiro, in *Framing the Social Security Debate,* edited by R. D. Arnold, M. J. Graetz, and A. H. Munnell, p. 364. See also *Social Security and Its Enemies,* by Max J. Skidmore, pp. 97–98.
26. "Myths and Misunderstandings about Public Opinion toward Social Security," by Lawrence R. Jacobs and Robert Y. Shapiro, in *Framing the*

Social Security Debate, edited by R. D. Arnold, M. J. Graetz, and A. H. Munnell, p. 356.

27. Ibid., p. 357.
28. For the data on confidence and support in this paragraph, see ibid., pp. 374–375, and "Strong Support but Low Confidence," by Virginia P. Reno and Robert B. Friedland, in *Social Security in the 21st Century,* edited by E. R. Kingson and J. H. Schulz, pp. 184–185.
29. For this result, see the NPR/ Kaiser/Kennedy School survey of May 20, 1999, Question 3.
30. "Myths and Misunderstandings about Public Opinion toward Social Security," by Lawrence R. Jacobs and Robert Y. Shapiro, in *Framing the Social Security Debate,* edited by R. D. Arnold, M. J. Graetz and A. H. Munnell, pp. 371–374, and "Social Security Politics and the Conflict Between Generations," by T. R. Marmor, F. L. Cook, and S. Scher, in *Social Security in the 21st Century,* edited by E. R. Kingson and J. H. Schulz, pp. 195–200.
31. "Myths and Misunderstandings about Public Opinion toward Social Security," by Lawrence R. Jacobs and Robert Y. Shapiro, in *Framing the Social Security Debate,* edited by R. D. Arnold, M. J. Graetz, and A. H. Munnell, p. 371. The data referred to are surveys conducted by DYG, Inc., for the AARP in 1985, 1995, and 1996.
32. "Strong Support but Low Confidence," by Virginia P. Reno and Robert B. Friedland, in *Social Security in the 21st Century,* edited by E. R. Kingson and J. H. Schulz, pp. 185–186.
33. Ibid., p. 378, fn. 29.
34. Question 24b. Similar results were obtained in a March 1999 NBC News/*Wall Street Journal* poll and a January 1999 *Los Angeles Times* poll.
35. See, for example, *The Social Security Primer,* by Wallace C. Peterson, pp. 152–162.
36. See "Will Social Security Be There for Me?" by R. J. Myers in *Social Security in the 21st Century,* edited by E. R. Kingson and J. H. Schulz, p. 209.
37. *Report of the National Commission on Social Security Reform,* chapter 2, p. 2.

CHAPTER ONE

1. Interview in *AARP Bulletin,* July-August 2001, p. 15.

2. Speech by President George W. Bush on May 2, 2001, as he introduced his newly appointed commission to reform Social Security.
3. See the *Status of the Social Security and Medicare Programs: A Summary of the 1999 Annual Reports,* by the Social Security and Medicare Boards of Trustees, March 31, 1999, and the *Report of the 1994–1996 Advisory Council on Social Security: Findings, Recommendations, and Statements,* pp. 1–2.
4. *Report of the 1994–1996 Advisory Council on Social Security: Social Security for the 21st Century,* p. 20. For the same view, see *Countdown to Reform,* by Henry Aaron and Robert Reischauer, p. 96. Also see the panel discussion "Social Security: It Ain't Broken," by Alicia Munnell, in *Social Security Reform,* edited by Steven Sass and Robert Triest, p. 298.
5. For discussions of these proposals, see, for example, *Straight Talk about Social Security,* by Robert Ball with Thomas Bethell, chapter 2; *Countdown to Reform,* by Henry Aaron and Robert Reischauer, chapter 6; *Should the United States Privatize Social Security?* by Henry Aaron and John Shoven, pp. 89–101; "Social Security in the Twenty-First Century," by C. Eugene Steuerle, in *Social Security in the 21st Century,* edited by Eric Kingson and James Schulz, pp. 247–257; and the *Report of the 1994–1996 Advisory Council on Social Security: Findings, Recommendations, and Statements.*
6. See the NPR/Kaiser/Kennedy survey of May 20, 1999, Question 21a, available at www.washingtonpost.com/wp-srv/politics/polls/polls.htm.
7. See *The Social Security Primer,* by Wallace Peterson, pp. 125–126.
8. See *Straight Talk about Social Security,* by Robert Ball with Thomas Bethell, pp. 24–25, Table 2.3.
9. See the *Report of the 1994–1996 Advisory Council on Social Security: Findings, Recommendations, and Statements,* pp. 8–9.
10. See *Social Security: A Primer,* Congressional Budget Office, September 2001, chapter 2, p. 7.
11. *Countdown to Reform,* by Henry Aaron and Robert Reischauer, p. 134.
12. The NPR/Kaiser/Kennedy survey of May 20, 1999, Question 21, available at www.washingtonpost.com/wp-srv/politics/polls/polls.htm
13. *Straight Talk about Social Security,* by Robert Ball with Thomas Bethell, pp. 24–25, Table 2.3.
14. See the *Status of the Social Security and Medicare Programs: A Summary of the 2001 Annual Reports,* by the Social Security and Medicare Boards of Trustees, March 19, 2001. There is no cap on the payroll tax for Medicare's

Hospital Insurance Trust Fund (HI), into which employee and employer each pay 1.45 percent.

15. *Straight Talk about Social Security,* by Robert Ball with Thomas Bethell, pp. 24–25, Table 2.3.
16. *The Social Security Primer,* by Wallace Peterson, p. 125.
17. *Social Security: The Phony Crisis,* by Dean Baker and Mark Weisbrot, p. 117.
18. See, for example, *The Social Security Primer,* by Wallace Peterson, appendix 3.
19. Ibid.
20. See, for example, *Countdown to Reform,* by Henry Aaron and Robert Reischauer, pp. 106–107; the *Report of the 1994–1996 Advisory Council on Social Security: Findings, Recommendations and Statements,* p. 10; and "Social Security in the Twenty-First Century," by C. Eugene Steuerle, in *Social Security in the 21st Century,* edited by Eric Kingson and James Schulz, p. 250.
21. *Report of the 1994–1996 Advisory Council on Social Security: Findings, Recommendations, and Statements,* p. 10.
22. Ibid.
23. *Straight Talk about Social Security,* by Robert Ball with Thomas Bethell, pp. 24–25, Table 2.3. See also *Countdown to Reform,* by Henry Aaron and Robert Reischauer, p. 107.
24. *Countdown to Reform,* by Henry Aaron and Robert Reischauer, p. 94.
25. See "Bridging the Centuries," by Robert Ball with Thomas Bethell, in *Social Security in the 21st Century,* edited by Eric Kingson and James Schulz, p. 272, Table 18.1.
26. See, for example, *The Social Security Primer,* by Wallace Peterson, p. 122, and appendix 3; and *Countdown to Reform,* by Henry Aaron and Robert Reischauer, pp. 104–105.
27. *The Social Security Primer,* by Wallace Peterson, p. 122.
28. See, for example, the devastating critique of the Boskin Commission's report in *Social Security: The Phony Crisis,* by Dean Baker and Mark Weisbrot, chapter 4. See also *Countdown to Reform,* by Henry Aaron and Robert Reischauer, p. 105.
29. *Report of the 1994–1996 Advisory Council on Social Security: Findings, Recommendations, and Statements,* p. 6.
30. *Straight Talk about Social Security,* by Robert Ball with Thomas Bethell, pp. 24–25, Table 2.3.

31. See, for example, *The Social Security Primer,* by Wallace Peterson, p. 76, or, in more detail, *Countdown to Reform,* by Henry Aaron and Robert Reischauer, Box 3–2 on p. 39.
32. *Report of the 1994–1996 Advisory Council on Social Security: Findings, Recommendations, and Statements,* p. 9. For a survey of reform plans including this proposal, see, for example, *The Social Security Primer,* by Wallace Peterson, appendix 3.
33. *Report of the 1994–1996 Advisory Council on Social Security: Findings, Recommendations, and Statements,* p. 9. See also *Straight Talk about Social Security,* by Robert Ball with Thomas Bethell, pp. 11–13, and *Countdown to Reform,* by Henry Aaron and Robert Reischauer, p. 104.
34. "Social Security in the Twenty-First Century," by C. Eugene Steuerle, in *Social Security in the 21st Century,* edited by Eric Kingson and James Schulz, pp. 248–249.
35. See *Straight Talk about Social Security,* by Robert Ball with Thomas Bethell, pp. 11–13, and *The Social Security Primer,* by Wallace Peterson, p. 123.
36. *Social Security: The Phony Crisis,* by Dean Baker and Mark Weisbrot, p. 111.
37. Ibid., pp. 112–113.
38. Ibid., p. 112.
39. See the NPR/Kaiser/Kennedy survey of May 20, 1999, Question 21, available at www.washingtonpost.com/wp-srv/politics/polls/polls.htm
40. See, for example, *The Social Security Primer,* by Wallace Peterson, appendix 3.
41. Specifically, starting in 2000 the normal retirement age increased from 65 by two months per year, so that it will reach 66 in 2005. It will remain 66 for 12 years and then increase again by two months per year to reach age 67 by 2022. See the *Report of the 1994–1996 Advisory Council on Social Security: Findings, Recommendations, and Statements,* p. 10.
42. After 2021, workers who retire at 62 will only receive 70 percent of their full benefit as compared with 80 percent currently. Ibid.
43. "At the rate of about 1 month every 2 years." The initial age of entitlement would remain at 62. Ibid.
44. *Report of the 1994–1996 Advisory Council on Social Security: Findings, Recommendations, and Statements,* p. 10.
45. *Report of the 1994–1996 Advisory Council on Social Security: Social Security for the 21st Century,* p. 35.

46. Ibid.
47. *Report of the 1994–1996 Advisory Council on Social Security: Social Security for the 21st Century,* p. 35.
48. Ibid.
49. *Washington Post National Weekly Edition,* June 5, 2000.
50. Ibid.
51. See the survey by NPR, the Kaiser Family Foundation, and Harvard University's Kennedy School of Government, taken in May of 1999. This is available at npr.org/programs/specials/poll/990518.ss1.html. See questions 15A and 15B.
52. For other plans that increase the normal retirement age see, for example, *The Social Security Primer,* by Wallace Peterson, appendix 3, and *Countdown to Reform,* by Henry Aaron and Robert Reischauer, p. 146 and the appendix.
53. See the *Report of the 1994–1996 Advisory Council on Social Security: Findings, Recommendations, and Statements,* p. 21, fn. 23.
54. See "Should Social Security Be Means-Tested?" by Eric Kingson and James Schulz, in *Social Security in the 21st Century,* edited by Eric Kingson and James Schulz, p. 47. A prominent advocate for means testing is Peter G. Peterson, a former secretary of Commerce. See, for example, his *Will America Grow Up before It Grows Old?* pp. 167–173.
55. *Report of the 1994–1996 Advisory Council on Social Security: Findings, Recommendations, and Statements,* p. 7. See also "Should Social Security Be Means-Tested? by Eric Kingson and James Schulz, in *Social Security in the 21st Century,* edited by Eric Kingson and James Schulz, pp. 52–53, and "Adequacy and Equity Issues: Another View," by Michael Hurd, in *Social Security in the 21st Century,* edited by Eric Kingson and James Schulz, pp. 220–221.
56. See, for example, *Countdown to Reform,* by Henry Aaron and Robert Reischauer, p. 118.
57. Ibid.
58. Ibid.
59. See *Social Security: The Phony Crisis,* by Dean Baker and Mark Weisbrot, p. 115.
60. See "Should Social Security Be Means-Tested?" by Eric Kingson and James Schulz, in *Social Security in the 21st Century,* edited by Eric Kingson and James Schulz, p. 55.
61. *Report of the 1994–1996 Advisory Council on Social Security: Findings, Recommendations, and Statements,* p. 2.

62. As an example of a money's worth calculation see the *Report of the 1994–1996 Advisory Council on Social Security: Social Security for the 21st Century,* p. 14, Figure 4.
63. See, for example, *The Social Security Primer,* by Wallace Peterson, p. 121.
64. *Report of the 1994–1996 Advisory Council on Social Security: Findings, Recommendations, and Statements,* p. 2.
65. I make the conventional assumption that raising taxes or cutting government spending would not be allowed by the Federal Reserve to depress total spending, for that would lower the nation's income as well as saving. To prevent a downturn in the economy resulting from increased taxes or reduced benefits, the Federal Reserve would be forced to lower interest rates, which would provide a stimulus for firms to undertake the additional investment projects referred to in the text. For a fuller discussion of this point, see *Deficit Hysteria,* by Arthur Benavie, chapter 3.
66. *Long-Term Budgetary Pressures and Policy Options,* by the Congressional Budget Office, May 1998, p. 6.
67. The argument in this paragraph holds for an increase in any tax rate, not just the payroll tax. It would also hold for any cut in government spending that is not public investment.
68. *Issues in Privatizing Social Security,* Report of an Expert Panel of the National Academy of Social Insurance, edited by Peter Diamond, p. 4.
69. *Report of the 1994–1996 Advisory Council on Social Security: Findings, Recommendations, and Statements,* p. 5.
70. For an analysis of this point, see *Deficit Hysteria,* by Arthur Benavie, chapter 3.
71. *Countdown to Reform,* by Henry Aaron and Robert Reischauer, p. 50.
72. Ibid.

CHAPTER TWO

1. See the George W. Bush official website, www.georgewbush.com.
2. Speech available at www.whitehouse.gov/news/releases/2002/02/20020228–3.html
3. See *The Social Security Primer,* by Wallace Peterson, appendix 3.
4. *Report of the National Commission on Social Security Reform,* chapter 2.
5. See "The Politics of Pensions: Lessons from Abroad," by Kent Weaver, in *Prospects for Social Security Reform,* edited by Olivia Mitchell, Robert Myers, and Howard Young, p. 200.

6. *Issues in Privatizing Social Security: Report of an Expert Panel of the National Academy of Social Insurance,* edited by Peter Diamond, p. 108.
7. See, for example, *Is It Time to Reform Social Security?* by Edward Gramlich, p. 68.
8. See, for example, Feldstein's op-ed piece entitled "Bush's Low-Risk Pension Reforms," which appeared in the *New York Times* on May 22, 2000.
9. Ibid.
10. See *Countdown to Reform,* by Henry Aaron and Robert Reischauer, p. 90.
11. *Should the United States Privatize Social Security?* by Henry Aaron and John Shoven, p. 169.
12. Ibid., p. 160.
13. Op-ed piece in the *New York Times,* May 26, 2000.
14. See "Bush's Do-It-Yourself Social Security Proposal," by Glenn Kessler in the *Washington Post National Weekly Edition,* May 22, 2000.
15. See Bush's official website, www.georgewbush.com.
16. "Restoring Security to our Social Security Retirement Program," by Joan Bok, Ann Combs, Sylvester Schieber, Fidel Vargas, and Carolyn Weaver in the *Report of the 1994–1996 Advisory Council on Social Security: Findings, Recommendations, and Statements,* p. 3.
17. "Social Security: Tune It Up, Don't Trade It In," by Henry Aaron in *Should the United States Privatize Social Security?* by Henry Aaron and John Shoven, pp. 68–69.
18. Op-ed piece in the *New York Times,* May 26, 2000.
19. *Countdown to Reform,* by Henry Aaron and Robert Reischauer, p. 74.
20. See "Social Security Money's Worth," by John Geanakoplos, Olivia Mitchell, and Stephen Zeldes, in *Prospects for Social Security Reform,* edited by Olivia Mitchell, Robert Myers, and Howard Young, pp. 100 and 139–140.
21. "Bridging the Centuries," by Robert Ball with Thomas Bethell, in *Social Security in the 21st Century,* edited by Eric Kingson and James Schulz, p. 283.
22. *Issues in Privatizing Social Security: Report of an Expert Panel of the National Academy of Social Insurance,* edited by Peter Diamond, p. 48.
23. *Countdown to Reform,* by Henry Aaron and Robert Reischauer, p. 36.
24. Ibid., p. 34, Box 3–1.
25. See "Restoring Security to our Social Security Retirement Program," by Joan Bok, Ann Combs, Sylvester Schieber, Fidel Vargas, and Carolyn Weaver, in the *Report of the 1994–1996 Advisory Council on Social Security: Findings, Recommendations and Statements,* p. 8.

26. See "Are Social Security Benefits Too High or Too Low?" by Marilyn Moon, in *Social Security in the 21st Century,* edited by Eric Kingson and James Schulz, p. 65, Table 4.1.
27. Ibid.
28. See, for example, *Countdown to Reform,* by Henry Aaron and Robert Reischauer, pp. 32–36; *Should the United States Privatize Social Security?* by Henry Aaron and John Shoven, pp. 62–66, and *Straight Talk about Social Security,* by Robert Ball with Thomas Bethell, pp. 43–45.
29. *Should the United States Privatize Social Security?* by Henry Aaron and John Shoven, p. 63.
30. *Countdown to Reform,* by Henry Aaron and Robert Reischauer, p. 34.
31. Ibid.
32. *Countdown to Reform (Revised and Updated),* by Henry Aaron and Robert Reischauer, pp. 33–37.
33. "New Opportunities for the Social Security System," by Stephen Kellison and Marilyn Moon, in *Prospects for Social Security Reform,* edited by Olivia Mitchell, Robert Myers, and Howard Young, pp. 69–70.
34. *Countdown to Reform,* by Henry Aaron and Robert Reischauer, pp. 86–88.
35. "Are Returns on Payroll Taxes Fair?" by Yung-Ping Chen and Stephen Goss, in *Social Security in the 21st Century,* edited by Eric Kingson and James Schulz, p. 77.
36. "Bridging the Centuries," by Robert Ball with Thomas Bethell, in *Social Security in the 21st Century,* edited by Eric Kingson and James Schulz, p. 276.
37. *Should the Unites States Privatize Social Security?* by Henry Aaron and John Shoven, pp. 72–73.
38. "The Risks of Pension Privatization in Britain," by James Schulz in, *Challenge,* January-February 2000, p. 99.
39. See, for example, "Investment and Administrative Constraints on Individual Social Security Accounts," by Robert Pozen and John Kimpel in *Prospects for Social Security Reform,* edited by Olivia Mitchell, Robert Myers, and Howard Young, pp. 372–379, and *Straight Talk about Social Security,* by Robert Ball with Thomas Bethell, pp. 49–56.
40. *Issues in Privatizing Social Security: Report of an Expert Panel of the National Academy of Social Insurance,* edited by Peter Diamond, p. 74.
41. Ibid., p. 126.
42. *Straight Talk about Social Security,* by Robert Ball with Thomas Bethell, pp. 50–52.

43. *Countdown to Reform,* by Henry Aaron and Robert Reischauer, pp. 88–89.
44. "A Political Science Perspective on Social Security Reform," by Hugh Heclo, in *Framing the Social Security Debate,* edited by R. D. Arnold, M. J. Graetz, and A. H. Munnell, p. 85.
45. *Countdown to Reform,* by Henry Aaron and Robert Reischauer, p. 89.
46. See, for example, ibid., p. 71, and *Issues in Privatizing Social Security: Report of an Expert Panel of the National Academy of Social Insurance,* edited by Peter Diamond, p. 91.
47. See, for example, *True Security,* by Michael Graetz and Jerry Mashaw, p. 43; and "Bridging the Centuries," by Robert Ball with Thomas Bethell, in *Social Security in the 21st Century,* edited by Eric Kingson and James Schulz, p. 276.
48. The 1999 *Report of an Expert Panel of the National Academy of Social Insurance,* pp. 20–21.
49. Ibid., p. 17.
50. "A Political Science Perspective on Social Security Reform," by Hugh Heclo in *Framing the Social Security Debate,* edited by R. D. Arnold, M. J. Graetz, and A. H. Munnell, p. 80.
51. *Countdown to Reform,* by Henry Aaron and Robert Reischauer, p. 42.
52. Ibid.
53. "Restoring Security to Our Social Security Retirement Program," by Joan Bok, Ann Combs, Sylvester Schieber, Fidel Vargas, and Carolyn Weaver, in the *Report of the 1994–1996 Advisory Council on Social Security,* pp. 17 and 29.
54. *The Social Security Primer,* by Wallace Peterson, p. 117.
55. "Social Security in the 21st Century," by Robert Ball et al. in the *Report of the 1994–1996 Advisory Council on Social Security,* p. 32.
56. See, for example, "Social Security: Tune It Up, Don't Trade It In," by Henry Aaron, in *Should the Unites States Privatize Social Security?* by Henry Aaron and John Shoven, p. 85, and *The Social Security Primer,* by Wallace Peterson, p. 117.
57. See "Bush's Do-It-Yourself Social Security Proposal," by Glenn Kessler, in the *Washington Post National Weekly Edition,* May 22, 2000.
58. Op-ed piece by Alan Blinder in the *New York Times,* May 26, 2000.
59. "Social Security Money's Worth," by John Geanakoplos, Olivia Mitchell, and Stephen Zeldes, in *Prospects for Social Security Reform,* edited by Olivia Mitchell, Robert Myers, and Howard Young, p. 124. See also "Individual Uncertainty in Retirement Income Planning under Different

Public Pension Regimes," by Lawrence Thompson, in *Framing the Social Security Debate,* edited by R. Douglas Arnold, Michael Graetz, and Alicia Munnell, pp. 152–153.

60. *Issues in Privatizing Social Security: Report of an Expert Panel of the National Academy of Social Insurance,* edited by Peter Diamond, p. 48.
61. See comment by Alicia Munnell in *Should the United States Privatize Social Security?* by Henry Aaron and John Shoven, pp. 135–136.
62. *Is It Time to Reform Social Security?* by Edward Gramlich, p. 7.
63. See "Social Security Privatization: A Structure for Analysis," by Olivia S. Mitchell and Stephen P. Zeldes, in *The American Economic Review,* May 1996, pp. 363–367; and "Proposals to Restructure Social Security," by Peter A. Diamond, in the *Journal of Economic Perspectives,* summer 1996, pp. 72–73.
64. *Is It Time to Reform Social Security?* by Edward Gramlich, p. 7.
65. *Straight Talk About Social Security,* by Robert Ball with Thomas Bethell, p. 46.
66. See, for example, *Countdown to Reform,* by Henry Aaron and Robert Reischauer, p. 77, and "Restoring Security to our Social Security Retirement Program," by Joan Bok, Ann Combs, Sylvester Scheiber, Fidel Vargas, and Carolyn Weaver in the *Report of the 1994–1996 Advisory Council on Social Security: Findings, Recommendations, and Statements,* p. 4.
67. Research cited by David Cutler in *Should the United States Privatize Social Security?* by Henry Aaron and John Shoven, p. 131.
68. See, for example, *Issues in Privatizing Social Security: Report of an Expert Panel of the National Academy of Social Insurance,* edited by Peter Diamond, p. 108, and "Social Security: In What Form?" by John Geanakoplos, Olivia Mitchell, and Stephen Zeldes, in *Framing the Social Security Debate,* edited by R. D. Arnold, M. J. Graetz, and A. H. Munnell, p. 150.
69. "Social Security Privatization: Experiences Abroad," a study by the Congressional Budget Office, January 1999, chapter 1, p. 2.
70. See, for example, "The United Kingdom's Pension Program," by Richard Disney, in *Social Security Reform,* edited by Steven Sass and Robert Triest, pp. 158–162.
71. Discussion by Richard Disney in *Framing the Social Security Debate,* edited by R. D. Arnold, M. J. Graetz, and A. H. Munnell, pp. 231–232.
72. See the discussion by Richard Disney, ibid., p. 230; and "The Politics of Pensions: Lessons from Abroad," by R. Kent Weaver, in *Framing the Social Security Debate,* edited by R. D. Arnold, M. J. Graetz, and A. H. Munnell,

p. 234. See also *Is It Time to Reform Social Security?* by Edward Gramlich, p. 76.

73. "The Politics of Pensions: Lessons from Abroad," by R. Kent Weaver in *Framing the Social Security Debate,* edited by R. D. Arnold, M. J. Graetz, and A. H. Munnell, pp. 235, 237, and 217. See also Richard Disney's discussion in the same book, p. 232.
74. *Social Security and Its Enemies,* by Max Skidmore, p. 4.
75. "The Risks of Pension Privatization in Britain," by James Schulz in *Challenge,* January-February 2000, pp. 93–94.
76. Ibid., p. 96.
77. "The Politics of Pensions: Lessons from Abroad," by R. Kent Weaver, in *Framing the Social Security Debate,* edited by R. D. Arnold, M. J. Graetz, and A. H. Munnell, p. 226.
78. "The Risks of Pension Privatization in Britain," by James Schulz, in *Challenge,* January-February 2000, p. 96.
79. "Individual Uncertainty in Retirement Income Planning under Different Public Pension Regimes," by Lawrence Thompson, in *Framing the Social Security Debate,* edited by R. D. Arnold, M. J. Graetz, and A. H. Munnell, p. 134.
80. "The Risks of Pension Privatization in Britain," by James Schulz, in *Challenge,* January-February 2000, p. 97.
81. Ibid.
82. This evidence of continued mis-selling is reported in Schulz, ibid., pp. 97–98.
83. Discussion by Richard Disney in *Framing the Social Security Debate,* edited by R. D. Arnold, M. J. Graetz, and A. H. Munnell, p. 231.
84. Ibid.
85. "The Risks of Pension Privatization in Britain," by James Schulz, in *Challenge,* January-February 2000, p. 98.
86. See, for example, "The Economics of Social Security Reform," by Peter Diamond, in *Framing the Social Security Debate,* edited by R. D. Arnold, M. J. Graetz, and A. H. Munnell, pp. 52–55.
87. Reported in "The Risks of Pension Privatization in Britain," by James Schulz, in *Challenge,* January-February 2000, p. 99.
88. "The Economics of Social Security Reform," by Peter Diamond, in *Framing the Social Security Debate,* edited by R. D. Arnold, M. J. Graetz, and A. H. Munnell, p. 54.
89. Reported in "The Risks of Pension Privatization in Britain" by James Schulz, in *Challenge,* January-February 2000, p. 99.

90. "Pension Choices and Pensions Policy in the United Kingdom," by David Blake, in *The Economics of Pensions,* edited by S. Valdes-Prieto, p. 289; and "The Risks of Pension Privatization in Britain," by James Schulz, in *Challenge,* January-February 2000, p. 99.
91. "The Risks of Pension Privatization in Britain," by James Schulz, in *Challenge,* January-February 2000, p. 100.
92. Ibid., p. 101.
93. Ibid., p. 104.
94. "The Politics of Pensions: Lessons from Abroad," by R. Kent Weaver, in *Framing the Social Security Debate,* edited by R. D. Arnold, M. J. Graetz, and A. H. Munnell, pp. 226–227.
95. See, for example, the Personal Security Account (PSA) plan favored by five members of the Advisory Council and described in "Restoring Security to Our Social Security Retirement Program," by Joan Bok, Ann Combs, Sylvester Schieber, Fidel Vargas, and Carolyn Weaver, in the *Report of the 1994–1996 Advisory Council on Social Security: Findings, Recommendations, and Statements.* Also, see the similar plan offered by the World Bank in *Averting the Old Age Crisis: Policies to Protect the Old and Promote Growth.* For a summary of a number of privatization proposals, see *The Social Security Primer,* by Wallace Peterson, appendix 3, and *Countdown to Reform,* by Henry Aaron and Robert Reischauer, chapter 7.
96. See "The Chilean Pension Reform: A Pioneering Program," by Sebastian Edwards, in *Privatizing Social Security,* edited by Martin Feldstein, pp. 37–38.
97. Ibid., p. 39.
98. Ibid., pp. 42–43.
99. See "Compliance in Social Security Systems around the World," by Joyce Manchester, in *Prospects for Social Security Reform,* edited by Olivia Mitchell, Robert Myers, and Howard Young, p. 304; and "An Actuary's Perspective," by Robert Myers, in *Social Security: What Role for the Future?* edited by Peter Diamond, David Lindeman, and Howard Young, p. 212.
100. See "The Chilean Pension Reform: A Pioneering Program," by Sebastian Edwards, in *Privatizing Social Security,* edited by Martin Feldstein, pp. 38–55; "Proposals to Restructure Social Security," by Peter Diamond in *The Journal of Economic Perspectives,* summer 1996, pp. 75–86; and *The Real Deal,* by Sylvester Schieber and John Shoven, pp. 315–316.
101. "Chile's Private Pension System at 18: Its Current State and Future Challenges," by L. Jacobo Rodriguez, a Cato Project on Social Security Privatization, July 30, 1999, p. 3.

102. This minimum is either 50 percent of the average return of all the AFPs or 2 percentage points below this average, whichever is higher. The maximum is defined analogously. See, for example, "The Chilean Pension Reform: A Pioneering Program," by Sebastian Edwards, in *Privatizing Social Security,* edited by Martin Feldstein, p. 44.
103. See "Chile's Private Pension System at 18: Its Current State and Future Challenges," by L. Jacobo Rodriguez, a Cato Project on Social Security Privatization, July 30 1999, pp. 15–16.
104. Ibid., p. 14, Table 13.
105. See, for example, "Proposals to Restructure Social Security," by Peter Diamond, in *The Journal of Economic Perspectives,* summer 1996, p. 76.
106. "The Chilean Pension Reform: A Pioneering Program," by Sebastian Edwards, in *Privatizing Social Security,* edited by Martin Feldstein, p. 47.
107. Ibid.
108. "Compliance in Social Security Systems around the World," by Joyce Manchester, in *Prospects for Social Security Reform,* edited by Olivia Mitchell, Robert Myers, and Howard Young, p. 304.
109. "An Economist's Perspective," by Peter Diamond, in *Social Security: What Role for the Future?* edited by Peter Diamond, David Lindeman, and Howard Young, p. 215.
110. Ibid., pp. 216–217.
111. Ibid., and "The Chilean Pension Reform: A Pioneering Program," by Sebastian Edwards, in *Privatizing Social Security,* edited by Martin Feldstein, p. 45.
112. See the summary of the discussion of Sebastian Edwards's paper in *Privatizing Social Security,* edited by Martin Feldstein, p. 61. For a summary of Friedland's report, see *Funding Social Security* by Lawrence Seidman, p. 105.
113. See for example "Bridging the Centuries" by Robert Ball with Thomas Bethell in *Social Security in the 21st Century,* edited by Eric Kingson and James Schulz, p. 286; and "An Actuary's Perspective," by Robert Myers, in *Social Security: What Role for the Future?* edited by Peter Diamond, David Lindeman, and Howard Young, p. 211.
114. See, for example, *Funding Social Security,* by Lawrence Seidman, p. 107.
115. See, for example, "An Actuary's Perspective," by Robert Myers, in *Social Security: What Role for the Future?* edited by Peter Diamond, David Lindeman, and Howard Young, p. 213; and the comment on Sebastian Edwards's paper by Stephen Zeldes in *Privatizing Social Security,* edited by Martin Feldstein, p. 59.

116. See "Bridging the Centuries," by Robert Ball with Thomas Bethell, in *Social Security in the 21st Century,* edited by Eric Kingson and James Schulz, p. 283; and the comment on Sebastian Edwards's paper by Stephen Zeldes in *Privatizing Social Security,* edited by Martin Feldstein, p. 59.
117. "The Chilean Pension Reform: A Pioneering Program," by Sebastian Edwards, in *Privatizing Social Security,* edited by Martin Feldstein, p. 55.
118. See, for example, "Bridging the Centuries," by Robert Ball with Thomas Bethell, in *Social Security in the 21st Century,* edited by Eric Kingson and James Schulz, p. 287; the comment on Sebastian Edwards's paper by Stephen Zeldes in *Privatizing Social Security,* edited by Martin Feldstein, p. 59; and "An Actuary's Perspective," by Robert Myers, in *Social Security: What Role for the Future?* edited by Peter Diamond, David Lindeman, and Howard Young, p. 213.
119. "Social Security: Tune It Up, Don't Trade It In," by Henry Aaron, in *Should the United States Privatize Social Security?* by Henry Aaron and John Shoven, p. 73. Kent Weaver makes a similar argument in "The Politics of Pensions: Lessons from Abroad," in *Framing the Social Security Debate,* edited by R. D. Arnold, M. J. Graetz, and A. H. Munnell, p. 227.
120. Remarks by the President in Social Security Announcement, May 2, 2001, available at www.whitehouse.gov/news/releases/2001/05/text/20010502.html
121. Ibid.
122. "A Finale in Three-Part Harmony," by Richard Stevenson, in the *New York Times,* December 12, 2001, p. A21; and "Commission Impossible," by Nicholas Confessore, in the *American Prospect,* December 17, 2001.
123. See the Lindsey quote in "Commission Impossible," by Nicholas Confessore, in the *American Prospect,* December 17, 2001.
124. "Strengthening Social Security and Creating Personal Wealth for All Americans," *Report of the President's Commission,* December 21, 2001, pp. 83 and 84.
125. "A Finale in Three-Part Harmony," by Richard Stevenson, in the *New York Times,* December 12, 2001.
126. *AARP Bulletin,* January 2002, p. 2.
127. The *Economist,* December 15, 2001, p. 24. For the magazine's support of privatization, see its January 12, 2002, issue, p. 11.
128. Editorial in the *New York Times,* December 27, 2001, p. A18.

129. "How to Fix Social Security (to Be Continued)," by Amy Goldstein, in the *Washington Post National Weekly Edition,* December 10–16, 2001, p. 29.
130. Ibid.
131. "Strengthening Social Security and Creating Personal Wealth for All Americans," *Report of the President's Commission,* December 21, 2001, p. 9.
132. See "Social Security Reform: The Questions Raised by the Plans Endorsed by President Bush's Social Security Commission," by Henry Aaron, Alicia Munnell, and Peter Orszag, Report by the Center on Budget and Policy Priorities, December 3, 2001, available at www.cbpp.org
133. Remarks by the President in Social Security Announcement, May 2, 2001, available at www.whitehouse.gov/news/releases/2001/05/text/20010502.html. In fact, the report is entitled "Strengthening Social Security and Creating Personal Wealth for All Americans."
134. "Strengthening Social Security and Creating Personal Wealth for All Americans," *Report of the President's Commission,* December 21, 2001, p. 56.
135. Ibid.
136. "Commission Impossible," by Nicholas Confessore, in the *American Prospect,* December 17, 2001, p. 1.
137. Op-ed, in the *New York Times,* March 5, 2002.
138. "Social Security Reform: The Questions Raised by the Plans Endorsed by President Bush's Social Security Commission," by Henry Aaron, Alicia Munnell, and Peter Orszag, Report by the Center on Budget and Policy Priorities, December 3, 2001, available at www.cbpp.org
139. "Undermining Social Security with Private Accounts," by Christian Weller, in EPI Issue Brief #172, December 11, 2001, available at www.epinet.org/issuebriefs/ib172.html
140. "Social Security Commission Proposals Contain Serious Weaknesses but May Improve the Debate in an Important Respect," by Robert Greenstein, December 26, 2001, Center on Budget and Policy Priorities, available at www.cbpp.org

CHAPTER THREE

1. See, for example, "Social Security for the 21st Century," by Robert Ball, Edith Fierst, Gloria Johnson, Thomas Jones, George Kourpias, and Gerald Shea in the *Report of the 1994–1996 Advisory Council on Social Secu-*

rity: Findings, Recommendations, and Statements, p. 30; or, "Thinking About Social Security's Trust Fund," by Kent Smetters, in *Prospects for Social Security Reform,* edited by Olivia Mitchell, Robert Myers, and Howard Young, p. 208.

2. *Countdown to Reform,* by Henry Aaron and Robert Reischauer, pp. 108–109.
3. See, for example, *The 2000 OASDI Trustees Report* from the Office of the Chief Actuary, p. 5 of *Highlights,* available at www.ssa.gov/OACT/TR/TR00/trib.html
4. "Social Security for the 21st Century," by Robert Ball, Edith Fierst, Gloria Johnson, Thomas Jones, George Kourpias, and Gerald Shea, in the *Report of the 1994–1996 Advisory Council on Social Security: Findings, Recommendations, and Statements,* p. 27.
5. Ibid., p. 26.
6. "Restoring Security to our Social Security Retirement Program" by Joan Bok, Ann Combs, Sylvester Schieber, Fidel Vargas, and Carolyn Weaver, in the *Report of the 1994–1996 Advisory Council on Social Security: Findings, Recommendations, and Statements,* p. 30.
7. See "Restoring Security to our Social Security Retirement Program" by Joan Bok, Ann Combs, Sylvester Schieber, Fidel Vargas, and Carolyn Weaver, in the *Report of the 1994–1996 Advisory Council on Social Security: Findings, Recommendations and Statements,* p. 31.
8. Ibid.
9. *The Real Deal,* by Sylvester Schieber and John Shoven, p. 348.
10. "Restoring Security to our Social Security Retirement Program," by Joan Bok, Ann Combs, Sylvester Schieber, Fidel Vargas, and Carolyn Weaver, in the *Report of the 1994–1996 Advisory Council on Social Security: Findings, Recommendations, and Statements,* p. 31.
11. See, for example, *The Real Deal,* by Sylvester Schieber and John Shoven, p. 127.
12. *Countdown to Reform,* by Henry Aaron and Robert Reischauer, pp. 110–111.
13. Ibid. See also "Social Security for the 21st Century," by Robert Ball, Edith Fierst, Gloria Johnson, Thomas Jones, George Kourpias, and Gerald Shea, in the *Report of the 1994–1996 Advisory Council on Social Security: Findings, Recommendations, and Statements,* p. 30.
14. See "Investing Public Money in Private Markets," by Theodore Angelis, in *Framing the Social Security Debate,* edited by R. Douglas Arnold, Michael Graetz, and Alicia Munnell, pp. 293–299.

15. See, for example, "Social Security for the 21st Century," by Robert Ball, Edith Fierst, Gloria Johnson, Thomas Jones, George Kourpias, and Gerald Shea, in the *Report of the 1994–1996 Advisory Council on Social Security: Findings, Recommendations, and Statements,* p. 29; and *Funding Social Security,* by Lawrence Seidman, pp. 50–51.
16. Ibid.
17. See the op-ed piece by Paul Krugman in the *New York Times,* August 21, 2001.
18. See, for example, *Countdown to Reform,* by Henry Aaron and Robert Reischauer, p. 111; *Funding Social Security,* by Lawrence Seidman, pp. 50–51; and "Macroeconomic Aspects of Social Security Reform," by Peter Diamond, in *Brookings Papers on Economic Activity 2,* p. 42.
19. See *True Security,* by Michael Graetz and Jerry Mashaw, pp. 263–264.
20. *The Social Security Primer,* by Wallace Peterson, pp. 113–114.
21. *Making Sense of Social Security Reform,* by Daniel Shaviro, pp. 122–123.
22. Ibid., p. 122.
23. See the *1999 Report of an Expert Panel of the National Academy of Social Insurance,* p. 65.
24. See "Thinking about the Social Security's Trust Fund" by Kent Smetters, in *Prospects for Social Security Reform,* edited by Olivia Mitchell, Robert Myers, and Howard Young, p. 207.
25. See *The Real Deal,* by Sylvester Schieber and John Shoven, p. 349; and "Public Pension fund Activism in Corporate Governance," by Roberta Romano, in the *Columbia Law Review,* May 1993, pp. 795–853.
26. *The Real Deal,* by Sylvester Schieber and John Shoven, p. 348.
27. Ibid., pp. 348–349.
28. "Public Pension Fund Activism in Corporate Governance," by Roberta Romano, in the *Columbia Law Review,* May 1993, pp. 795–853.
29. "Investing Public Money in Private Markets," by Theodore Angelis, in *Framing the Social Security Debate,* edited by R. Douglas Arnold, Michael Graetz, and Alicia Munnell, p. 290, fn 8, originally reported in the *Wall Street Journal,* February 22, 1989, p. C1.
30. "Investing Public Money in Private Markets," by Theodore Angelis, in *Framing the Social Security Debate,* edited by R. Douglas Arnold, Michael Graetz, and Alicia Munnell, p. 292. See also James White, "Picking Losers: Back Yard Investing Yields Big Losses, Roils Kansas Pension System," *Wall Street Journal,* August 21, 1991, p. A1.
31. *The Real Deal,* by Sylvester Schieber and John Shoven, p. 350.

32. See, for example, *Countdown to Reform,* by Henry Aaron and Robert Reischauer, p. 111; *Funding Social Security,* by Lawrence Seidman, pp. 50–51; and "Macroeconomic Aspects of Social Security Reform," by Peter Diamond, in *Brookings Papers on Economic Activity 2,* p. 42.
33. *Countdown to Reform,* by Henry Aaron and Robert Reischauer, p. 111.
34. Remarks by Peter Diamond in a panel discussion in *Social Security Reform,* Federal Reserve Bank of Boston, 1997, edited by Steven Sass and Robert Triest, p. 290.
35. *The Real Deal,* by Sylvester Schieber and John Shoven, p. 350.
36. Ibid.
37. "Investing Public Money in Private Markets," by Theodore Angelis, in *Framing the Social Security Debate,* edited by R. Douglas Arnold, Michael Graetz, and Alicia Munnell, pp. 302–303.
38. "Thinking about Social Security's Trust Fund," by Kent Smetters, in *Prospects for Social Security Reform,* edited by Olivia Mitchell, Robert Myers, and Howard Young, p. 206. See the quote by Karl Borden.
39. *Countdown to Reform,* by Henry Aaron and Robert Reischauer, p. 108.
40. *The Great Deficit Scares,* by Robert Eisner, p. 46.
41. Ibid., p. 45–46.
42. Ibid., p. 46.
43. *Social Security and Its Enemies,* by Max Skidmore, pp. 82–83.
44. *Making Sense of Social Security Reform,* by Daniel Shaviro, p. 96.
45. *Countdown to Reform* (Revised and Updated for 2001), by Henry Aaron and Robert Reischauer, p. 117.
46. *Report of the 1994–1996 Advisory Council on Social Security: Findings, Recommendations and Statements,* p. 7.
47. Ibid., p. 8.
48. Ignoring the 3 percent that comes from the income taxation of Social Security benefits.
49. For Roosevelt's statement, see *Funding Social Security,* by Laurence S. Seidman, pp. 153–154.
50. *Countdown to Reform,* by Henry Aaron and Robert Reischauer, p. 109.
51. See, for example, *The Social Security Primer,* by Wallace Peterson, p. 124.
52. Ibid., p. 116. See also "Social Security in the Twenty-First Century," by C. Eugene Steuerle, in *Social Security in the 21st Century,* edited by Eric Kingson and James Schulz, p. 250.
53. See, for example, *Social Security: The Phony Crisis,* by Dean Baker and Mark Weisbrot, p. 118.

54. See *The Social Security Primer,* by Wallace Peterson, appendix 3; and in *Countdown to Reform,* by Henry Aaron and Robert Reischauer, chapter 7 and the appendix.
55. See the *Economic Report of the President,* February 1999, p. 33.
56. Reported in the *Economist,* October 7, 2000, pp. 34–35.
57. Under a budget deficit, excess payroll taxes reduce the Treasury's need to borrow from the public—that is, sell Treasury bonds to the public. If these payroll taxes were used by the trust fund to buy private securities instead of Treasury bonds, the Treasury would lose that revenue and would increase its borrowing from the public. Consequently, diversification would increase the Treasury bonds held by the public, and reduce the Treasury bonds held by the trust fund, whatever the state of the overall budget.
58. See "What Economic Role for the Trust Funds?" by Barry Bosworth, in *Social Security in the 21st Century,* edited by Eric Kingson and James Schulz, p. 171.
59. "Thinking about Social Security's Trust Fund," by Kent Smetters, in *Prospects for Social Security Reform,* edited by Olivia Mitchell, Robert Myers, and Howard Young, p. 207, and "Social Security for the 21st Century," by Robert Ball, Edith Fierst, Gloria Johnson, Thomas Jones, George Kourpias, and Gerald Shea, in the *Report of the 1994–1996 Advisory Council on Social Security: Findings, Recommendations, and Statements,* p. 30.
60. See the *1999 Report of an Expert Panel of the National Academy of Social Insurance,* p. 82.
61. For Greenspan's remarks, see "A Framework for Considering Social Security Reform," by Michael Boskin, in *Framing the Social Security Debate,* edited by R. Douglas Arnold, Michael Graetz, and Alicia Munnell, p. 49.
62. "Investing Public Money in Private Markets," by Theodore Angelis, in *Framing the Social Security Debate,* edited by R. Douglas Arnold, Michael Graetz, and Alicia Munnell, p. 314.

BIBLIOGRAPHY

Aaron, Henry J. "Social Security: Tune It Up, Don't Trade It In," in *Should the United States Privatize Social Security?* by Henry Aaron and John Shoven. Cambridge: MIT Press, 1999.

Aaron, Henry J., Alicia Munnell, and Peter Orszag. "Social Security Reform: The Questions Raised by the Plans Endorsed by President Bush's Social Security Commission," Report by the Center on Budget and Policy Priorities, December 3, 2001.

Aaron, Henry J. and Robert D. Reischauer. *Countdown to Reform.* New York: Century Foundation Press, Revised and Updated, 2nd ed., 2001.

Aaron, Henry J., and Robert D. Reischauer. *Countdown to Reform.* New York: Century Foundation Press, 1998.

Aaron, Henry J., and John B. Shoven. *Should the United States Privatize Social Security?* Cambridge: MIT Press, 1999.

Angelis, Theodore. "Investing Public Money in Private Markets," in *Framing the Social Security Debate,* edited by R. Douglas Arnold, Michael Graetz, and Alicia Munnell. Washington, D.C.: National Academy of Social Insurance, 1998.

Arnold, R. Douglas, Michael J. Graetz, and Alicia H. Munnell, eds. *Framing the Social Security Debate.* Washington, D.C.: National Academy of Social Insurance, 1998.

Baker, Dean, and Mark Weisbrot. *Social Security: The Phony Crisis.* Chicago: University of Chicago Press, 1999.

Ball, Robert M., with Thomas N. Bethell. *Straight Talk about Social Security.* New York: Century Foundation Press, 1998.

Ball, Robert M., with Thomas N. Bethell. "Bridging the Centuries," in *Social Security in the 21st Century,* edited by E. R. Kingson and J. H. Schulz. New York: Oxford University Press, 1997.

Ball, Robert, Edith Fierst, Gloria Johnson, Thomas Jones, George Kourpias, and Gerald Shea. "Social Security for the 21st Century," in the *Report of the 1994–1996 Advisory Council on Social Security: Findings, Recommendations and Statements.* Washington, D.C.: Advisory Council on Social Security, 1997.

Benavie, Arthur. *Deficit Hysteria.* Westport, Conn.: Praeger Publishers, 1998.

Bergmann, Barbara R. *Is Social Security Broke?* Ann Arbor: University of Michigan Press, 2000.

Berkowitz, Edward. *America's Welfare State From Roosevelt to Reagan.* Baltimore: Johns Hopkins University Press, 1991.

Blake, David. "Pension Choices and Pensions Policy in the United Kingdom," in *The Economics of Pensions: Principles, Policies, and International Experience,* edited by S. Valdes-Prieto. Cambridge, U.K.: Cambridge University Press, 1997.

Bok, Joan, Ann Combs, Sylvester Schieber, Fidel Vargas, and Carolyn Weaver. "Restoring Security to our Social Security Retirement Program," in the *Report of the 1994–1996 Advisory Council on Social Security: Findings, Recommendations and Statements.* Washington, D.C.: Advisory Council on Social Security, 1997.

Boskin, Michael J. "A Framework for Considering Social Security Reform," in *Framing the Social Security Debate,* edited by R. D. Arnold, M. J. Graetz, and A. H. Munnell. Washington, D.C.: National Academy of Social Insurance, 1998.

Bosworth, Barry. "What Economic Role for the Trust Funds?" in *Social Security in the 21st Century,* edited by Eric Kingson and James Schulz. New York: Oxford University Press, 1997.

Cavanaugh, Francis X. *The Truth About the National Debt.* Boston: Harvard Business School Press, 1996.

Chen, Yung-Ping, and Stephen Goss. "Are Returns on Payroll Taxes Fair?" in *Social Security in the 21st Century,* edited by Eric Kingson and James Schulz. New York: Oxford University Press, 1997.

Confessore, Nicholas. "Commission Impossible," in the *American Prospect,* December 17, 2001.

Congressional Budget Office (CBO). *Social Security: A Primer.* Washington, D.C.: U.S. Government Printing Office, 2001.

Congressional Budget Office. *The Economic and Budget Outlook: Fiscal Years 1998–2007.* Congress of the United States, January 1997; *The Economic and Budget Outlook: An Update.* July 1999; and *The Economic and Budget Outlook: Fiscal Years 2001–2010.* January 2000. Washington, D.C.: U.S. Government Printing Office.

Congressional Budget Office study. "Social Security Privatization: Experiences Abroad," Washington, D.C.: U.S. Government Printing Office, January 1999.

Congressional Budget Office, *Long-Term Budgetary Pressures and Policy Options.* Washington, D.C.: U.S. Government Printing Office, May 1998.

Diamond, Peter A., ed. *Issues in Privatizing Social Security: Report of an Expert Panel of the National Academy of Social Insurance.* Cambridge: MIT Press, 1999.

Diamond, Peter A. "The Economics of Social Security Reform," in *Framing the Social Security Debate,* edited by R. D. Arnold, M. J. Graetz, and A. H. Munnell. Washington, D.C.: National Academy of Social Insurance, 1998.

Diamond, Peter A. "Macroeconomic Aspects of Social Security Reform," in *Brookings Papers on Economic Activity 2,* 1997.

Diamond, Peter A. "Proposals to Restructure Social Security," in the *Journal of Economic Perspectives,* summer 1996.

Diamond, Peter A. "An Economist's Perspective, in *Social Security: What Role for the Future?* edited by Peter Diamond, David Lindeman, and Howard Young. Washington, D.C.: National Academy of Social Insurance, 1996.

Diamond, Peter A., David C. Lindeman, and Howard Young, eds. *Social Security: What Role for the Future?* Washington, D.C.: National Academy of Social Insurance, 1996.

Disney, Richard. "The United Kingdom's Pension Program," in *Social Security Reform,* edited by Steven Sass and Robert Triest.

Edwards, Sebastian. "The Chilean Pension Reform: A Pioneering Program," in *Privatizing Social Security,* edited by Martin Feldstein.

Eisner, Robert. *The Great Deficit Scares.* New York: Century Foundation Press, 1997.

Feldstein, Martin, ed. *Privatizing Social Security.* Chicago: University of Chicago Press, 1998.

Geanakoplos, John, Olivia Mitchell, and Stephen Zeldes. "Social Security Money's Worth," in *Prospects for Social Security Reform,* edited by Olivia Mitchell, Robert Myers, and Howard Young. Philadelphia: University of Pennsylvania Press, 1999.

Graetz, Michael J., and Jerry L. Mashaw. *True Security.* New Haven, Conn.: Yale University Press, 1999.

Gramlich, Edward M. *Is It Time to Reform Social Security?* Ann Arbor: University of Michigan Press, 1998.

Greenstein, Robert. "Social Security Commission Proposals Contain Serious Weaknesses but May Improve the Debate in an Important Respect," Center on Budget and Policy Priorities, December 26, 2001.

Heclo, Hugh. "A Political Science Perspective on Social Security Reform," in *Framing the Social Security Debate,* edited by R. D. Arnold, M. J. Graetz and A. H. Munnell. Washington, D.C.: National Academy of Social Insurance, 1998.

Jacobs, Lawrence R., and Robert Y. Shapiro. "Myths and Misunderstandings about Public Opinion toward Social Security," in *Framing the Social Security Debate,* edited by R. D. Arnold, M. J. Graetz, and A. H. Munnell. Washington, D.C.: National Academy of Social Insurance, 1998.

Kellison, Stephen, and Marilyn Moon. "New Opportunities for the Social Security System," in *Prospects for Social Security Reform,* edited by Olivia Mitchell, Robert Myers, and Howard Young. Philadelphia: University of Pennsylvania Press, 1999.

Kingson, Eric R., and James H. Schulz, eds. *Social Security in the 21st Century.* New York: Oxford University Press, 1997.

Kingson, Eric R., and James H. Schulz. "Should Social Security Be Means-Tested?" in *Social Security in the 21st Century,* edited by Eric Kingson and James Schulz. New York: Oxford University Press, 1997.

Manchester, Joyce. "Compliance in Social Security Systems Around the World," in *Prospects for Social Security Reform,* edited by Olivia Mitchell, Robert Myers, and Howard Young. Philadelphia: University of Pennsylvania Press, 1999.

Marmor, Theodore R., Fay Lomax Cook, and Stephen Scher. "Social Security Politics and the Conflict Between Generations," in *Social Security in the 21st Century,* edited by E. R. Kingson and J. H. Schulz. New York: Oxford University Press, 1997.

Mitchell, Olivia S., Robert J. Myers, and Howard Young, eds. *Prospects for Social Security Reform.* Philadelphia: University of Pennsylvania Press, 1999.

National Commission on Social Security Reform. *Report of the National Commission on Social Security Reform.* Washington, D.C.: U.S. Government Printing Office, 1983.

Peterson, Peter G. *Will America Grow Up Before It Grows Old?* New York: Random House, 1996.

Peterson, Wallace C. *The Social Security Primer.* Armonk, N.Y.: M. E. Sharpe, 1999.

Pozen, Robert, and John Kimpel. "Investment and Administrative Constraints on Individual Social Security Accounts," in *Prospects for Social Security Reform,* edited by Olivia Mitchell, Robert Myers, and Howard Young. Philadelphia: University of Pennsylvania Press, 1999.

Reno, Virginia P., and Robert B. Friedland. "Strong Support but Low Confidence," in *Social Security in the 21st Century,* edited by E. R. Kingson and J. H. Schulz. New York: Oxford University Press, 1997.

Report of the 1994–1996 Advisory Council on Social Security. Vol. 1. Washington, D.C.: Advisory Council on Social Security, 1997.

Rodriguez, L. Jacobo. "Chile's Private Pension System at 18: Its Current State and Future Challenges," a Cato Project on Social Security Privatization.

Romano, Roberta. "Public Pension Fund Activism in Corporate Governance," in the *Columbia Law Review,* May 1993.

Sass, Steven A., and Robert K. Triest, eds. *Social Security Reform.* Conference Series No. 41. Federal Reserve Bank of Boston, 1997.

Scheiber, Sylvester J., and John B. Shoven. *The Real Deal.* New Haven, Conn.: Yale University Press, 1999.

Schulz, James. "The Risks of Pension Privatization in Britain," in *Challenge,* January-February 2000.

Seidman, Laurence S. *Funding Social Security.* Cambridge, U.K.: Cambridge University Press, 1999.

Shaviro, Daniel. *Making Sense of Social Security Reform.* Chicago: University of Chicago Press, 2000.

Skidmore, Max J. *Social Security and Its Enemies.* Boulder, Colo.: Westview Press, 1999.

Smetters, Kent. "Thinking About Social Security's Trust Fund," in *Prospects for Social Security Reform,* edited by Olivia Mitchell, Robert Myers, and Howard Young. Philadelphia: University of Pennsylvania Press, 1999.

Social Security Administration. *Basic Facts,* Publication No. 05–10080, January 2001.

Status of the Social Security and Medicare Programs: A Summary of the 2001 Reports, by the Social Security and Medicare Boards of Trustees, March 19, 2002.

Steuerle, C. Eugene. "Social Security in the Twenty-First Century," in *Social Security in the 21st Century,* edited by Eric Kingson and James Schulz. New York: Oxford University Press, 1997.

Strengthening Social Security and Creating Personal Wealth for All Americans, Report of the President's Commission, December 21, 2001.

Valdes-Prieto, Salvador, ed. *The Economics of Pensions: Principles, Policies, and International Experience.* Cambridge, U.K.: Cambridge University Press, 1997.

Thompson, Lawrence. "Individual Uncertainty in Retirement Income Planning under Different Public Pension Regimes," in *Framing the Social Security Debate,* edited by R. Douglas Arnold, Michael Graetz, and Alicia Munnell. Washington, D.C.: National Academy of Social Insurance, 1998.

Weaver, Kent. "The Politics of Pensions: Lessons from Abroad," in *Prospects for Social Security Reform,* edited by Olivia Mitchell, Robert Myers, and Howard Young. Philadelphia: University of Pennsylvania Press, 1999.

INDEX